# THE COLORFUL STORY OF
# NORTH AMERICAN
# INDIANS

# THE COLORFUL STORY OF
# NORTH AMERICAN
# INDIANS

## Royal B. Hassrick

**OCTOPUS**
Octopus Books

# CONTENTS

1
THE ORIGINS

2
THE DESERT DWELLERS

3
THE WOODLAND
INDIANS

4
FARMERS
OF THE MIDWEST

5
WARRIORS OF THE PLAINS

6
GATHERERS
OF THE FAR WEST

7
SEAFARERS OF
THE NORTHWEST COAST

8
HUNTERS OF THE NORTH

9
INDIANS OF TODAY

Suggested Reading Page 142/Index Page 143
Acknowledgements Page 144

First published 1974 by Octopus Books Limited
59 Grosvenor Street, London W1
ISBN 0 7064 0360 6
© 1974 Octopus Books Limited
Produced by Mandarin Publishers Limited
Quarry Bay, Hong Kong    Printed in Hong Kong

**Page 1** Shell gorget from the Etowa Mounds of Georgia. The eagle-like figure exhibits striking resemblance in costume to the Toltec and Mayan cultures of Mexico **Previous pages** An oil painting by Charles Russell entitled *The Horse Thieves*. A successful raid could bring wealth and prestige **Left** A Plains Indian travois, after an engraving by Frederic Remington **Right** Counting Coup. The first man to strike or "count coup" on an enemy earned the most credits

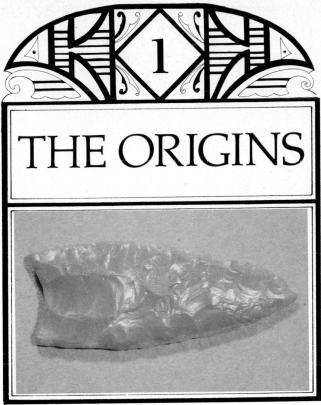

# 1

# THE ORIGINS

In the mists of a long and forgotten past, possibly as much as 50,000 years ago, men, tiny groups of hunters, small families, began to leave northern Asia. They moved toward the rising sun, exploring, yet more likely following game across the land bridge that once connected Siberia to what is now Alaska.

It was during the warm interglacial periods of the Pleistocene Age that parts of what are now arctic tundra were, in fact, quite lush and could support a variety of animal life. Such were the mammoths and mastodons, the early horse and other animals not associated with frigid climes. A vestigial form of humpless camel remained in South America as the llama and alpaca, but the mammoths and mastodons became extinct at the end of the Pleistocene, some 12,000 years ago.

It may well have been the ancient mammoth with its massive tusks and bounteous supply of meat that lured the daring hunters to Alaska. Armed only with rudimentary spears, the men had to attack and kill these huge beasts if they were to survive. And survive they did, this despite the fact that they did not yet know how to make fire.

As the centuries passed, more and more hunters came, first in driblets, then possibly in droves. Later, so much later as to be considered recent, men introduced the bow and arrow, a complicated invention which far surpassed the spear and *atlatl* as an effective

**Left** "Spruce Tree House"; Indian cliff dwellings in Mesa Verde National Park
**Above** A Clovis spearpoint attesting to an early civilization

weapon. As new people arrived, those who had come earlier were pushed, or more probably driven, farther and farther inland. Over a period of 20,000 years, scattered groups of men camped here and there throughout the entire continent of America.

At Santa Rosa, an island off the coast of California, dressed mammoth bones have been found in what appears to have been a barbecue pit. Radio carbon dating estimates them to be around 29,650 years old. Possibly by this time man had discovered how to make fire. In a cave at Sandia, New Mexico, a mammoth tusk has been dated at more than 20,000 years. Distinctive stone spearpoints, named for the site where they were discovered, exhibit a single shoulder form. Points like this have been found as far distant as Alabama and Alberta. In the Sandia cave the bones of prehistoric and now extinct camels, horses and mastodons were also found.

At Clovis, New Mexico, featherlike stone points as well as bone points have been discovered in association with the remains of mammoths which have been assigned a date of 15,000 years by some scholars. In Nevada, at Gypsom Cave, an atlatl or wooden spear thrower was discovered in association with the extinct giant sloth. It is believed these monstrous beasts were herded in pens by the early men. Again, a date between 8000 and 10,000 years ago has been assigned for these people.

As the years passed, other men appeared and with them followed the dog, their first domesticated animal. In all probability the dog tamed himself, scavenging around the campsites. But man learned that this animal could be of inestimable help, not only as an aid in hunting, but as a beast of burden. The relationship proved mutually invaluable.

With the ending of the glacial period, the elephants and saber-toothed tigers, the camels and horses disappeared. At Folsom, New Mexico, a beautifully worked fluted point was found wedged in the rib of a *Bison Antiqus*, a huge and now extinct variety of the American buffalo. Folsom points, dated as 8000 years old, have been found throughout the Great Plains from Texas to Alberta.

The people who migrated to the New World were not all of one kind, and while the ancestors of the Indians were predominately mongoloid with the characteristic black hair, brown eyes and tawny skin, there were many variations. Some were tall while others were stocky, some were longheaded, others round, some were quite fair-skinned, others very dark.

**Left** This deer mask from Key Marco, Florida, is a masterpiece of native sculpture **Above** A Mimbres bowl. These ceramics were ceremonially "killed" by punching a hole in them before placing them in graves **Below** An effigy bowl of diorite from an Alabama mound

And they brought with them various languages. Six distinct language families have been isolated which can give clues as to the successive waves of population. The dialects within a single family group are more often than not unintelligible from one tribe to another. As for differences between families, some are as diverse as Japanese is from Portuguese.

At Bat Cave, New Mexico, rudimentary maize—a primitive corn that popped—has been discovered dating back some 5000 to 6000 years. But by now the Southwest had become a vast desert marked by stark mesas, brilliant and dry against the searing sun. And yet it appears most likely that here the first attempts at agriculture north of Mexico took place. Concurrently, yet far to the north and east in the forest lands of the Great Lakes, men were fashioning tools of copper: spearpoints, axes, knives and chisellike celts. Possibly the hammered copper points were designed for arrows, the bow and arrow perhaps by now having been introduced from the North.

A thousand years elapsed and in the desert lands of the Southwest descendants of the early Cochise

**Above** A wooden deer mask from an Oklahoma mound **Right** A Hohokam bowl, an example of the first decorated pottery, c. 300 BC
**Above right** Basketmaker sandals were as handsome as they were practical
**Far right** A Pueblo woman's embroidered *manta*

farmers of Bat Cave built pit houses near their fields. Here they cultivated not only a variety of corn, but beans and squash. Around 300 B.C. the women made the first decorated pottery, now identified as Mogollon and Hohokam. By A.D. 1000, the latter had devised an impressive system of canals for irrigating their crops and had gradually moved from the pit houses to great tiered buildings of stone and adobe.

To the north of the Mogollon and Hohokam people there appeared another group of farmers referred to as Anasazi or "Ancient Ones." At about the time of Christ, these people, too, raised crops of corn, beans and squash. Theirs was a basketmaking culture, but by A.D. 500 they also had learned the art of pottery making. Within the following 800 years, these people likewise left their pit houses and began constructing masonry dwellings. By A.D. 1000, possibly for defense against marauding Athabascan-speaking people—Navaho and Apaches—the Anasazi retreated from the open country of Arizona and New Mexico, Utah and Colorado and built great fortified towns. These they

made safe in the majestic rock cliffs along the canyons that cut the region, and for nearly three centuries the people at Mesa Verde, Betatkin and Canyon de Chelly flourished. Others, rather than seeking refuge in the cliffs, built huge storied apartments of cut stone as a defense against their enemies. Like the cliff dwellers, the people at Aztec and Chaco Canyon, New Mexico, also thrived.

Known as the Great Pueblo period, the people of this time were now skillful farmers. They raised a variety of corn, both flour and flint in many colors, as well as squash, beans and cotton. They domesticated the turkey and kept eagles and colorful macaws imported from Mexico for their plumage. The men tilled the fields, hunted the small game, deer and rabbits. They also wove mantas, which they embroidered, and diamond- and twill-pattern shawls and dresses for the women, kilts and sashes for their own costumes. The ancient pit houses had now become circular ceremonial rooms or *kivas*. It was in these that the men held clan meetings and emerged from them as the masked gods or *kachinas* to perform ritualistic dances before the people.

The Pueblo women ground the corn in stone *manas* and fashioned handsome decorated pottery in black and white geometric designs. All except the people at Mimbres who embellished their pottery with whimsical life forms—men, birds and animals.

And then, almost mysteriously, the spectacular cliff dwellings, the fabulous circular cities, like Chaco Canyon, were abandoned. Evidence suggests that a cruel drought lasting over a period of twenty years combined with severe erosion forced the Pueblo farmers to search out new locations where they could find water for their crops. All this happened about A.D. 1250.

Far to the east of the arid lands of the Mogollons and Hohokams lay the dank forest regions of the Mississippi valley and the woodlands of the Southeast. Here

pottery has been discovered which is believed to have been made over 4000 years ago. Unlike the vessels of the Southwest which were painted, this was decorated with a kind of engraving called stamping. And it was a decorative form that was to dominate the entire eastern two-thirds of North America.

The discovery of pottery some 2500 years older than that of the Southwest suggests that very early these Indians were practicing agriculture and most probably living in permanent communities. Pottery, used both for cooking and the storage of grains and dried vegetables like beans and corn, is not readily transportable and its presence suggests a sedentary way of life. Only with an agricultural economy can such a community exist.

Here in the Mississippi valley and its tributaries the centuries passed. It wasn't until about 400 B.C. that any significant culture manifested itself. Now, from the Gulf as far west as Kansas, north to Wisconsin and east to New York, men began building burial mounds, sometimes in the form of an animal effigy. At Hopewell, Ohio, the finding of handsome stone-carved pipes in the form of animals and birds attest to their skill as artisans. From copper traded from the Great Lakes they fashioned large snake-head ornaments and double-headed birds. From mica, too, they made similar forms, many of which were sewn to their clothing. Little is known about the cause for the widespread influence of the mound builders. Whether a new religious concept or a confederation of intertribal traders or some other factors inspired this development is not yet known. Whatever the cohesive force, it appears to have been a strong one, for it lasted for over 800 years.

**Below** and **above** (in miniature) A model of the spectacular circular city of Chaco Canyon, huge storied apartments of cut stone built as a defense against enemies **Right** A stone effigy pipe from Spiró mound

At a much later date, far to the south, people living along the waterways that flow into the Mississippi acquired a combination of cultural traits with a distinct flavor of the people of Yucatan and the Toltecs of Mexico. As early as A.D. 1300, temples were being erected atop large earth pyramids, diminutive replicas of the great Mayan, Toltec and Aztec edifices. These Temple Mound people perpetually maintained a sacred fire in their temples, built their towns around a ceremonial plaza, cleaned their villages once a year. They appointed priests to guard the idols in their temples, carried their kings and nobles on litters, often maintained a rigid caste system and always hideously tortured their war captives. So many southern traits combine to suggest not only influence, but very likely a colonization by southerners themselves.

It was among these Temple Mound people that a strange and macabre Death Cult was either developed or introduced. Again and again there appear in their shell and copper ornaments motifs of skulls, men with weeping eyes, a single weeping eye and vultures. No one knows yet what it implied, but the obsession for what appears completely morbid at least suggests a slight preoccupation with the subject. Maybe they were scared to death. In any case, the cult was relatively short-lived and itself died out as mysteriously as it was born. The Temple Mound complex, however, continued, though in diminished form, into the early eighteenth century, among such groups as the Natchez and Apalachee, the Chitimacha, the Creeks and Cherokee and Caddos. And were it not for the European conquerors determined to destroy everything Indian, it might exist today.

Examples of Indian artistry
**Right** A Santo Domingo jar of handsome
proportion and design
**Below** Navaho silver squash blossom necklace
embellished with turquoise
**Far right** A Zuni bowl which combines
geometric, floral and animal motifs
**Below right** This Two Grey Hills rug is a
masterpiece of Navaho weaving

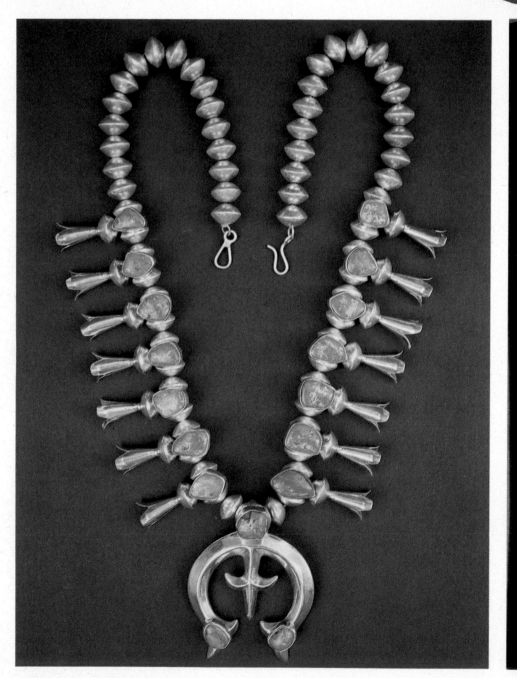

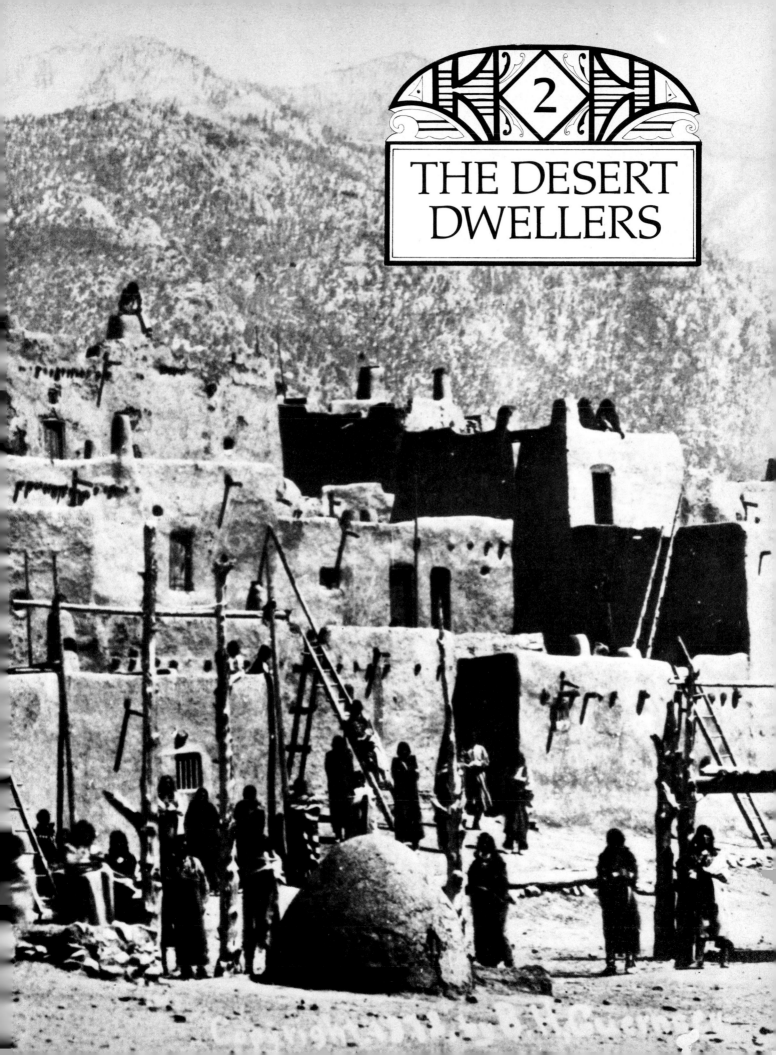

# 2

# THE DESERT DWELLERS

At the time of Columbus there dwelt in the Southwest many native groups exhibiting a variety of life-styles. Far to the south, in what is now southern Arizona, were the Pima and Papago, descendants, without much doubt, of the ancient Hohokam and Mogollon farmers. Nor had their life changed greatly from that of their ancestors.

To have selected so arid a region as a place to farm at first appears inconceivable. Here the rainfall averages only about thirteen inches a year and when the rains do come they are often as cloudbursts filling the normally dry washes with surging torrents of water. But actually, the Pimans didn't choose the land. Their ancestors, the Cochise, chose it and the Pimans just stayed.

Like their forefathers, they cultivated crops of corn, beans and pumpkins, but now had added cotton. The edible staples were supplemented by many wild fruits and berries, cactus buds and mesquite together with the meat of rabbits, deer, bear, antelope and the bighorn sheep. The Pimans lived in scattered villages, early in semisubterranean pit houses, later in upstanding, solid-walled structures. They wove blankets of rabbit skins, the men favoring skin ponchos and shirts of cotton, the women aprons of woven yucca fiber. They smoked clay pipes and even cigarettes, fashioned handsome pottery and superbly woven baskets.

The government was simple, unstructured and entirely democratic. A council of elders might choose one from among themselves as leader. Since tribal decisions demanded the unanimous agreement of the council, a principle that held true for the great majority of tribes throughout America, the chief was in reality the "voice" of the council.

**Previous pages** Taos Pueblo, one of America's oldest continually inhabited apartment complexes
**Left** A Pueblo craftsman drilling a bead
**Above right** Members of the Sia Giant Society curing a sick boy
**Right** Kachina dancers played an important part in Pueblo ceremony
**Far right** The Shalakos, giant Zuni Kachinas, dance to bless the new houses

These were a peaceful people having learned to live in harmony with themselves and rarely going to battle save in self-defense. So abhorrent was war that a returning warrior who had taken a scalp had to blacken his face in shame and be ceremonially purified.

To the northeast along the Rio Grande River flowing through New Mexico lay the towns of the great Pueblos. They, too, were experienced farming peoples, descendants of the Anasazi and the Cliff Dwellers. These were America's apartment house dwellers. And to their west were other villages, the Acoma, Zuni and Hopi, high atop shimmering mesas, those fabled landmarks of the Southwest.

Theirs was a life of toil and ceremony and peace. As the men labored in the fields, often far distant from the village, with their digging sticks and hoes, the women ground corn and made handsome painted pottery, now in multicolors. Like their forefathers, the men wove the textiles for garments and hunted deer and rabbits, sometimes alone, other times in groups, driving rabbits before them and killing them with throwing clubs.

As farming was a man's summer occupation, weaving was his winter task. On an upright loom he wove cotton dresses with diamond and diagonal twill patterns. For himself he made white kilts in simple tabby weave and embroidered the borders with red and black geometric designs.

The tradition of basketmaking among the Pueblos is an ancient one, dating as far back as the Basketmakers, in fact long before the Pueblos ever dreamed of apartment dwelling. The early Basketmakers wove sandals of yucca fiber and made basketry vessels woven so tightly that they could be used for cooking—throwing in hot stones to make the water boil. Dyed in mute colors, bundles of grass were coiled to make trays with whirlwind, kachina and geometric designs. Baskets of wicker were designed as trays, dishes, even cradles. Today, except among the Hopis, the art of basketry has disappeared from the Pueblos.

Pueblo pottery was made by coiling rolls of moist clay one upon the other, to form a dish or bowl. Smoothed with a wooden paddle, the vessel was fired in a kiln composed of a pile of dried wood stacked over the pot. When the firing was completed, the pot was smoothed and polished with a round stone. Next it was painted. The designs, most often geometric, were achieved freehand, the artisans' designs always coming out amazingly symmetrical without any trial sketching.

While all pottery was low-fired and hence porous, some was burnished with stone to assume a brightly polished effect. Some, like the Santa Clara water jars, had a symbolic bear's paw impressed near the rim, for it was the bear who first led the people to water. The porosity of the jars permitted moisture to reach the outside surface which, in the arid climate of the desert Southwest, evaporated rapidly, thus cooling the water.

Whether at Taos, the most northerly of the Rio Grande Pueblos, which rises as much as four stories

high against the backdrop of the Taos Mountains, or at Hopi, the most westerly of the Pueblos perched high on the edges of their barren mesas, the people's lives followed a regimen as certain as the seasons.

Spring was the time of planting and ceremonies were held to insure the germination of the seeds. More ceremonies, formal songs and dances by men representing the gods accompanied by rows of female attendants helped insure rain, so essential in a land of little rainfall. Harvesttime required more propitiation, blessing new houses still more. Among the Zuni, the giant *Shalako kachinas* performed. These towering gods, attired in eagle-feathered cloaks with great clacking beaks, danced before the populace. The womenfolk prepared sumptuous feasts of corn bread, meats and vegetables for anyone who might drop in. These life-renewing ceremonies were a colorful, festive and happy period, for the Pueblos, although industrious and reverent, were also a happy people.

Among their hierarchy of many gods were the "Fun Makers," the clowns. It was they, in their black-and-white-striped painted bodies and horned masks or as earth-daubed figures called "Mud Heads," who spoofed and ridiculed a delinquent member of the community. To the point of obvious shame, they frightened and scolded a naughty child or pantomimed the foibles of men, even jesting in lusty antic at the sexual activities of the people, a subject otherwise tabooed in a prim and proper society.

The Pueblos were very prim and proper. Conformity to the norm was demanded for the good of all; individuality was suspect, dangerous, if not evil. The ceremonies themselves were variations on the theme of life renewal. Subtle differences in costuming, in song, in dance steps were designed to fit the occasion.

To the untutored, the ceremonial dancing consisted of a monotonous ballet composed of strange masked gods and a long line of women wearing colorful *tablitas* chanting repetitious words in a singsong monotone for hours on end. And as a result, the rains came, the corn sprouted, the harvests were gathered. The Pueblo people had a system that was tried and true. Any deviation might spell disaster while strict adherence to custom had proved effective for hundreds of years.

As early as eight years of age Pueblo boys were harshly initiated into the realm of the supernatural by being thoroughly thrashed by the kachinas, not as punishment, but to cleanse and purify them. Sometime later boys were introduced to the mysteries of the kivas, learned something of the secrets of the clans, the roles of the gods, the meaning of the ceremonies. And they learned their duties with respect to them.

The kivas were the seat of Pueblo government. Generally owned by the clans, it was here the priests met. In some Pueblos, like Hopi and Zuni, men inherited the exalted positions, in others men voluntarily entered the realm of priesthood. In any case, men studied and became versed in the tribal rituals, the lore of the ancient gods, the skills of curing the sick. It

was these men who became the leaders, the *caciques* of the Pueblos and as such the rulers of the theocracies.

Sickness, as among all peoples, was a fearsome matter. In general, it was the priests who specialized in curing. This was attended by much ceremony, for only through supplication could the sickness be exorcised. Before an elaborate altar, offerings and an intricately complex earth painting of colored sand, the patient sat facing the doctor-priest, who by means of chants endeavored to remove the cause of the illness.

All life was patterned in Pueblo society; the time to plant the crops, the time to harvest, the time for boys to learn the system of things. And then there were the ceremonies, scheduled, regimented, and embellished with dances as precise as a row of chorus girls. Life was orderly, life was secure, life was happy, albiet anything but democratic. For the Pueblos, change and progress were dangerously abhorrent, frighteningly risky. Yet unlike so many striving, ambitious, lustful and daring nations bent on expansion and progress, the Pueblos had the achieved answer—very simply, they had arrived.

It is believed by some authorities that Athabascan speakers, men from the north, invaded the territory of the Great Pueblos, possibly as early as A.D. 700, probably as small marauding bands of hunting warriors. No one really knows. They called themselves "Diné," the "People," and their warlike ferocity may have been the cause of the Anasazi's building fortlike dwellings under the protection of the huge south-western cliffs.

Their descendants, the Navaho and Apache of New Mexico and Arizona, surrounded the Pueblos in their own country. As hunters they brought with them a powerful, newly designed bow—one reinforced with sinew—as well as a better method of arrow release. The simple method of holding the arrow's nock against the bowstring pinched between the thumb and fore-finger was now improved by pressing the nock against the side of the forefinger and then using the tips of the third and fourth fingers to pull against the bowstring. Equipped with these technical improvements, the Athabascans became efficient hunters and effective raiders, no doubt delighting in the pillage of the Pueblos' crops.

The history of the Apaches is that of a warlike group. Living in scattered camps composed of brush-covered *wickiups* giving the appearance of a bristling, overturned basket, they completely ravished the countryside. Stealthy stalking and sudden raid were their manner of attack. Success was measured in booty and glory.

Some of the Apaches tended small gardens and it was generally the women who raised the crops. The women also made baskets, watertight canteens covered with pitch, as well as coiled storage bins and trays of willow and devil's claw. These were handsomely decorated either in geometric patterns or human and animal motifs. When the men weren't raiding, they hunted deer, rabbits and small game.

Each year they held a "Coming Out" party for the young girls who had reached puberty. Elaborately attired in painted and beaded costumes fringed with dangling cones of jingling tin, the young women made music as they danced at their presentation. Strange masked dancers representing gods of the four directions—East, West, North and South—and a small boy personifying the invisible spirit of the Great Spirit blessed the young girls.

Unlike the Pueblos, the Apaches were anything but theocratic. Leadership was dependent solely upon individual initiative—some men were more or less granted a position of authority, others merely assumed it by personal dominance.

To the north and west of Apache country was the land of the Navaho. These hunters seemed slightly milder in nature than their Apache cousins, a little more willing to adopt the ways of their peaceful neighbors, the Pueblos. From them they not only learned the techniques of farming, but weaving, basketmaking, and, moreover, even embraced aspects of their religion. From the Spanish and Mexicans they acquired the knowledge of sheepherding and the skills

**Left** Hopi women grinding corn. The squash blossom hairdo of the girl on the right signifies that she is unmarried **Right** A Jicarilla Apache girl wearing a beaded deerskin cape, kept for special occasions

**Right** A painting by H. B. Molehausen showing
Navaho Indians **Below** The blanket of a
Navaho chief. Often considered the most
colorful of all American Indians, the Navaho
are still famous for their crafts

of silversmithing. So able, so willing were the Navahos
to incorporate the techniques of their neighbors and
then add to them a special quality of their own that
today they are considered one of the most colorful of
all American Indians.

In small log huts, later daubed and chinked with
clay, the Navaho lived in scattered communities
nestled along the hidden waterways which cut the
deep, red sandstone canyons of the Southwest. Young
men and boys tended little flocks of sheep and hunted
small game, while the women wove woolen textiles on
an upright loom copied from the Pueblos. They made
dresses, black with red borders similar to the Pueblos,

but instead of a single wraparound blanket, the Navaho fashioned two smaller rectangles and then stitched them together to form a simple tube. Around their waists they wore a belt of silver conchos and, as foot covering, bootlike moccasins which buttoned up the sides with silver buttons. Both men and women adorned themselves with shining silver necklaces and bracelets.

A style of necklace conceived and especially favored by the Navaho is referred to as the "Squash Blossom." Silver beads are interspersed with silver blossoms, while at the base of the necklace an inverted horseshoe-shaped device called a *naja* is suspended. This striking piece of jewelry has a fascinating history, which proves it to be, with the exception of the idea of beads, wholly European. The art of silversmithing was learned from a Mexican. The squash blossoms are in reality miniature pomegranates, a Spanish symbol of hope and devotion. The naja is an ancient Moorish emblem to ward off the evil eye, and was brought to the New World by the Spanish who used it as a horse trapping on their bridles. And yet the Navaho combined these foreign concepts to create something so unique, so Navaho that there can be no question that the Squash Blossom necklace is completely Indian.

Today, not only do the Navaho men make silver

25

necklaces, they make rings and bracelets and "bow guards" often set with handsome blue and blue green turquoise. They have even mastered the art of sand casting, especially suited to massive openwork bracelets in geometric curvilinear patterns.. And the Navaho make great use of their jewelry, bedecking themselves with silver, necklace upon necklace, rings on every finger, bracelets upon bracelets. Such a gaudy display is a sign of status and prosperity.

If the Navaho men are master silversmiths, the women are master weavers. Observing their skill, American traders during the later nineteenth century capitalized upon it by encouraging the women to adapt their weaving of dresses and blankets to the making of rugs. Bartering with flour, cheap velveteen, canned beans and slab bacon for a fine woven rug, the traders got rich. And yet, without their encouragement, the small home industry which has produced some of

the most unique and handsome rugs the world has ever seen might never have occurred.

From the early native "Chief's Blankets" with their bold bars of red, black and white to the subtle geometric designs and muted colors of vegetable-dyed yarns of the "Wide Ruins," the Navaho rug is a masterpiece. Over the years different styles developed in the remote communities. At Two Grey Hills, for example, bold geometric forms woven with natural black, brown and white wool were popular while at Ganado the rugs are noted for their deep red backgrounds overlain by stark black and white geometric patterns.

The Navaho are still a highly religious people awed by sickness and death. Unlike the Pueblos whose ceremonies center around the forces of nature which affect the growth of their crops, the Navaho as a traditional hunting people, seem more concerned with

Masked Apache dancers representing the four directions. The boy personifies the invisible spirit of the Great Spirit

the well-being of the individual. Illness is a fearsome matter and their ceremonies are devoted to its cure. Cures are effected by employing the services of a "chanter" or priest versed in the songs of his people's mythology. The ceremony lasts eight days and when performed in accordance with tradition, a new lodge is erected. Here the patient is brought. On the floor, the chanter and his assistant prepare a sand painting, reminiscent of the Pueblo, though far more elaborate and beautiful. Colored sands are sifted through the thumb and forefinger to produce exquisitely delicate symbols depicting the gods of mythological times. When complete it becomes, in fact, an altar upon which the patient is seated as the ceremony proceeds. Here offerings are made, songs are sung, all to the purpose of cleansing the patient and infusing him with the health-giving powers of the supernaturals. When this phase of the rite is finished, the painting is destroyed. On the final night, powerful masked dancers perform as spirits as does a clown. Other men perform tricks such as sleight of hand and on occasion an arrow swallower may appear. The curing is not without its cost. The patient must offer a feast to the performers and guests and pay the chanter and his helpers in jewelry, sheep or other articles of value. Yet for the patient, this is a time of joy and celebration—the gods have shared their power and he is well again.

The first European ever seen by the Indians of the land of the shimmering mesas was one Estevanico, a black Spanish slave from Morocco. Leading troops of Indians from Mexico, he stumbled upon a village of Zunis. Not only did he advise them of other strangers to follow, including a man who was white, but in typical Spanish fashion demanded tribute both in turquoise and in women. The Zuni elders counciled long and finally came to a drastic solution. They forthrightly filled him with arrows and left him dead. Those of his troops who escaped hastened to report to the others who were following. They, too, including the white Spanish friar, turned heel and fled to Mexico.

But the Spanish were determined. The lure of gold and the urgency to convert savage infidels to Christianity was an obsession. In the spring of 1540, under

**Above** Hastobiga, a Navaho shaman or medicine man **Right** A Navaho arrow swallower who would probably be present at ceremonies for curing the sick

the leadership of Don Francisca Vasques de Coronado, they again attempted to invade the land of the Pueblos. Again the Zunis were confronted, but this time not only by white soldiers in shining armor, but by strange and unheard-of beasts—the horse.

Coronado promptly demanded their surrender which was just as quickly refused. Again and again the Spaniard pleaded, but the Zunis were defiant. At last the Spanish leader's patience ended and the village was attacked. In the fighting that ensued, the Indians pelted Coronado's helmet so vigorously with rocks that he was carried unconscious from the battle. Yet within an hour the village of Hawiku was conquered. And from that moment on the life-style of the Pueblos would never be quite the same.

In the following autumn a large force of men and women, cattle, sheep, pigs and goats invaded the country. Those villages which would not surrender were ravaged by the Spanish soldiers. Blankets and food were commandeered, even the Pueblo women. And those who would not submit to the foreigners' indignities were summarily killed. The Spanish were acting like the bigoted pillagers they really were.

When summer came, Coronado commenced an expedition to the fabled golden cities of Quivira. Blinded by the brilliance of imagined wealth, the conquistador led his army through the trackless plains of Texas. First meeting what were probably Apaches, buffalo hunters in skin-covered tents, he proceeded as far north as what is now Kansas. Here he observed sadly and was thoroughly shocked by the simple grass lodges of the Wichita, a Caddoan-speaking farming group. The hoped-for wonders of Quivira had eluded him and he returned discouraged, so much so that he made his way straight to Mexico taking with him all the Spaniards and their domestic stock. All except two friars who remained to Christianize the Indians. Their proselytizing was short-lived as both Franciscans were promptly killed.

It was not until 57 years later that the Spanish seriously attempted again to impose themselves upon the Indians. Then Juan de Oñate led 400 settlers and 7000 head of livestock to the Southwest. Most of the Pueblos remembered the wrath of the Spaniard and the price of defiance. Not so the Acomas. Perched high on a mesa, the residents of the "Sky City" resisted. But as at Zuni years before, the Spanish, here scaling the seemingly impregnable cliffs, very quickly overcame the Acomas. They killed the men and took 500 women and children captive. What few men did survive were condemned to slavery and as if to insure it, Oñate ordered that one of their feet be cut off.

As the years went by, the conquerors continued to demand tribute—euphemistically called taxes—plunged the Indians into slavery, threw them into prison for recalcitrance and imposed their insistent Christian friars on the villages. But through it all the Pueblos retained their Indian ways—their economy, their family life and, to the consternation of the Franciscans, their native religious ceremonies.

Nearly a century of subjugation had passed when an Indian named Popé was released from jail at the colonial capital of Santa Fe. So incensed, so bitter was this man of the San Juan Pueblo that he brooded and schemed and then devised a brilliant plan. By organizing each Pueblo to concerted action, he believed the Indians could drive out the invaders and rid the land of a veritable plague. It was no simple matter to win unanimity among divergent peoples, but Popé's enthusiasm prevailed. The Pueblos arose in unison. They killed the friars and burned the churches and drove before them the 2000 Spanish settlers. They rousted the Spanish governor from his adobe palace at Santa Fe, and killed about 500 palefaces.

The revolt was a complete success, but a short one. In 1692, only twelve years after the uprising, the indomitable Spaniards returned. Within four years they had reestablished their oppression.

A kind of resigned acceptance to European domination prevailed in the Southwest. As the Spanish settlements became more firmly established, the Pueblos overtly accepted the tenets of Catholicism while still practicing the ancient tribal ceremonies not only secretly in their subterranean kivas, but openly in their town plazas. And the friars finally had wit enough to see that the Indians were very smart—that they could readily add Christian precepts to their own native beliefs. If one set of gods were effective, what harm in adding the Father, Son and Holy Ghost? Certainly the Spaniards, in conquering them, had superior gods. Surely the Pueblos could use all the help they could get.

It wasn't until 1848 when the United States acquired New Mexico and Arizona from Mexico that the balance of power changed in the Southwest. Up until this time the Apaches had been having great fun raiding the Pueblos and Spanish settlements. Nor were the Navahos opposed to pilfering sheep and horses and goats. But they were a little more inclined to make friends than the Apaches. They had even harbored Pueblo people during the period of Spanish plundering and from them learned many skills. Not so the Apaches. They had suffered too much from the ruthlessness of the Spaniards and were ever resentful of the callous white man. Now they must contend with the Americans.

In 1863 Colonel Kit Carson was ordered to bring the Navahos to peace and this he did most expeditiously. Rather than trying to overcome them militarily, he and his troops systematically killed their flocks of sheep, destroyed their crops of corn and peaches. Within a year the Navahos, starved to the point of surrender, flocked to Fort Defiance some 8000 strong. For four long years they were kept prisoner at Fort Sumner along the Pecos River of New Mexico. And then by the Treaty of 1868, in return for a promise never to defy the authority of the United States, they were returned to their homeland. Here they were given sheep in replacement for those destroyed, supplied with tools and clothes and schools for their children. And yet, while over a century has since elapsed, the Navahos have not forgotten the horrible sadness of "Fort."

The marauding Apaches were like wary wolf packs, harassing settlers, miners and travelers with a canny slyness. Led by men like Cochise, they were hard to find, hard to shoot and hard to kill. Only at the conclusion of the Civil War in 1865 did the United States make a concerted effort to control their resistance. And only after costly campaigns aimed at their complete annihilation were the Apaches partly subdued, eventually to be placed on reservations throughout Arizona and New Mexico.

Their treatment under government jurisdiction was at first pitiful. Forced upon reservations in areas they said they did not like, existing on short-change rations on which unscrupulous suppliers got rich, the Apaches suffered humiliation and absolute hunger. In the mid-1870s their resentment flared. Geronimo, a wily and artful warrior, assumed leadership of a small band of Chiricahua and raised terror throughout the region. When he finally surrendered to General Nelson Miles in 1894, he and his people were shipped to Florida and confined in the bastions of the ancient Spanish fort at St. Augustine. Later removed to Oklahoma, their imprisonment ended in 1913.

Today, the Southwest retains much of its Indian flavor. Indians still carry on their colorful ceremonies. The Pueblos fashion handsome pottery and jewelry, the Navaho create striking silver pieces and weave beautiful rugs. The Pimas and Papagos continue to practice their art of basketry. Though tarnished by early conquest and present-day commercialism, the land of the desert mesas is still most enchanting and still quite Indian. The aura of the Anasazi, "The Ancient Ones," continues to pervade the atmosphere.

Geronimo, the intrepid Apache headman who fought long to preserve his people's freedom

# 3
# THE WOODLAND INDIANS

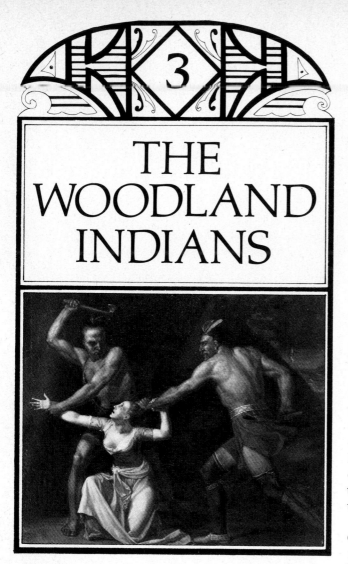

The eastern woodlands of North America were a dense, verdant and often impenetrable forest wilderness cut by rivulets, streams and deep rivers. The Appalachian Mountains stretch, steep and rugged, north and south. In the 1500s it was a region lush with wild fruits and vegetables. Grapes and cherries and persimmons, onions, potatoes and artichokes grew in profusion. Rich, too, was the supply of wild game. Deer, bear, rabbits and wildfowl abounded—even the small woodland buffalo. The creeks and rivers were rich with fish as well as clams and oysters.

The Indians who dwelt here, from the Tunica in semitropical Florida to the Penobscot in frigid Maine, were farming people. Like the Indians of the Southwest, they raised crops of corn, beans and squash, but unlike the Southwesterners it was the women who tilled the fields. And the agricultural methods were different, too. Instead of permanent fields, they cleared the forests by slashing the bark from the tree trunks and burning them. In this way they carved out little fields which they assigned to the women and their families. The method of slash and burn, emanating from far to the south—Mexico and even Yucatan—depleted the soil. Despite the fact that they fertilized, commonly placing a fish in each hill of corn, the fields wore out. Generally, after about fifteen years the fields were impoverished, the crops declined and the Indians simply moved their villages to start anew.

The Indians of Florida were a majestic people. Their kings, resplendent in their very nakedness, ruled with the power of a benevolent despot. Their queens, highly honored, were borne on litters attended by maidens in waiting. They waged wars, wars in which no quarter was given. By scalping, mutilating, hacking off the arms and legs of their captives, they destroyed any chance of their enemies' evil power contaminating the spirit world.

In the 1500s, the Calusa were most powerful. As early as 1513 a fleet of seagoing canoes, manned by Calusa warriors, drove off the ships of Ponce de León. Parenthetically, avaricious Ponce just couldn't give up. He was not only hunting for gold, but for the Fountain of Youth, both at the expense of the Indians. He never found either, but did receive a fatal poisoned dart in the back, shot from a blowgun by an Indian disturbed by his blatant trespassing.

The proud Tunicas, first encountered by the French, later became pawns of the Spanish. Like the Apalachee to the north, who were eventually crushed by the Creeks under English domination, the Tunicas were completely subdued by the mid-eighteenth century. Here in Florida began a pattern whereby European contestants played natural Indian enemies one against the other to their ultimate defeat and in this instance to their total annihilation.

North of Florida, along the coastlines of the Carolinas and Virgina, English explorers, as early as 1584, first met the people of Pomeiok and later the Pamlico. Said Captain Arthur Barlow of them, "We found these people gentle, loving and faithful, lacking all guile and trickery. It was as if they lived in a golden age of their own."

Typical of the eastern seaboard people of this time were the Algonquian-speaking Powhatans who welcomed Captain John Smith and his Jamestown colonists in 1607. Powhatan, the king, had carved himself a small empire. From his seat at the falls of the James River, now Richmond, Virginia, he controlled nearly all the tidewater country and received homage from some 200 villages. Powhatan was not only powerful, but exceedingly wealthy from the tribute he received in hides and corn and freshwater pearls. From his vassals Powhatan could muster a considerable force of warriors. With them he could conquer and plunder town after town. First with a surprise attack of flaming arrows setting fire to the mat-covered wigwams, the warriors then subdued the victims in hand-to-hand fighting with murderous war clubs.

**Above** A painting by John Vanderlyn depicting the death of Jane McCrea at the hands of Indians **Right** A chief of the Pamlico, after a painting by John White

painting them selues when
they goe to their generall
huntings or at theire
Solemne feasts.

While some of the villages were open and unprotected, the majority were stockaded. Here the fields were located beyond the palisades where the women raised several varieties of corn including dent, flint and even popcorn. They also grew several forms of squash, beans and tobacco. These they not only enjoyed freshly cooked from the gardens, but they dried and stored great quantities in underground caches against wintertime. To this diet was added all manner of dried fruits, wild vegetables and roots. Meat, too, was a staple, deer being especially favored, while fish caught in weirs were relished.

Clothing was made by the women, themselves wearing a skin apron, a string of shell beads and little more. The men dressed much the same. Softly tanned deerskin robes and turkey-feathered mantles added warmth in winter. Powhatan himself owned a great cape of buffalo hide ornamented with shells.

Women wore their hair long over the shoulders, while the men shaved the side of the heads leaving an upright crest or roach down the center. This they embellished with feathers. Pearls, worn at the ear lobes, were especially prized as adornments, as were plates of copper suspended from the neck.

The Powhatans believed in a multiplicity of supernatural spirits called *mantoacs* and a supreme power or *Manatou* which controlled the universe. Great reverence was accorded the ancestors. The mummified remains of tribal leaders or *weroans* were preserved and guarded in a special house. Powhatan's house was in reality a temple. At the rear, in the shadows of an unlit room, sat a carved image of a man—in truth, the likeness of the gods.

While at first Powhatan welcomed the colonists at Jamestown, even offering food to the struggling settlement, tensions and misunderstandings developed. Several weroans, particularly one *weroanqua*, or queen, and Powhatan's own brother, Opechancanough, were both strongly opposed to the white man's encroachment. At one point, John Smith was captured and brought before Powhatan. His life was barely saved by "Frisky," Powhatan's daughter who, legend records, threw her body over the English captive. Later, she herself was captured and held hostage by the governor at Jamestown on the pretense of keeping the peace. Familiarly known as Pocahontas, she was christened and married at the age of seventeen to one John Rolfe. It was generally agreed that by her various acts of conciliation she was really instrumental in maintaining the transitory peace. Pocahontas was taken to London where she was feted. Because her father, Powhatan, was the only foreign personage ever to be accorded sovereignty by England, Pocahontas was raised to the elevation of nobility. Eligible for an audience with the queen, she was received by Elizabeth, while John Rolfe, a commoner, stayed in the wings. Pocahontas bore John Rolfe one son, and she died of smallpox in England at the age of twenty-one.

At her death and that of her father's shortly after, Opechancanough assumed power. Much bloodshed followed and in 1622 the English colony was reduced to a mere 350 souls. And yet, over a period of 40 years, the white man prevailed. In a series of retaliatory attacks, the Indians were decisively overcome. By 1650 the Powhatans were crushed, dispersed and impoverished.

.II.

R. Saturioua

Three scenes of Indian life by the artist,
Jacques Le Moyne **Far left** Florida Indians
hunting deer **Above** A Timuca headman exhorts
his allied chiefs to war **Left** The bride-to-be
of a Timuca king is carried to her wedding

All along the Atlantic seaboard, from Virginia to
Maine, the Algonquian-speaking peoples held sway.
In what is now New Jersey and eastern Pennsylvania,
the Leni Lenapi or Delawares were dominant. Their
way of life, though similar to that of the Powhatans,
was far less stylized, far less formal. They had no
hereditary kings, but leaders, elected in council from
among the elders.

Such a one was Lapowinsa, a Delaware leader who
treated with William Penn in the "Walking Purchase"
of 1686 for as much land as a man could cover in a day
and a half. For over 50 years Lapowinsa kept his word
and so did Penn. But then, in 1737, unscrupulous
land-hungry men, wanting more territory, convinced
the Delawares to negotiate another Walking Treaty.
This time, however, instead of one man walking, three
men ran, covering some 60 miles to the Pocono
Mountains. Cheated, the Delawares acquiesced and
sadly gave up their lands.

35

**Left** John White's painting of the stockaded
town of Pomeiok in North Carolina
**Above** Algonquian Indians of the Atlantic
Seaboard celebrated victories with singing
accompanied by rattles

And so it was all along the eastern seaboard from New
York to Massachusetts. The Manhatts, a subtribe of
the Delawares, were euchred out of Manhattan Island
by the Dutch for a mere 24 dollars. Seventeen years
later, the Wappinger Indians, of which the Manhatts
were probably a part, sought refuge from marauding
Mohawks in New Amsterdam, now New York City.
The Indians were at first given protection by the
Dutch governor, but after a few days were suddenly
ambushed at night by their very protectors. The Dutch
brought eight trophy heads of men, women and children to the fort together with other captives. Here one
Indian was brutally tortured and mutilated, much to
the gleeful laughter of the pantalooned and fork-
tongued governor himself. The Europeans were showing their color—white—and white was now equated
with treachery and evil.

In Massachusetts the Wampanoags, or rather their
remnants, first met the Pilgrims in 1620. They had
been a populous nation, numbering some 10,000 souls,
only to be decimated by a plague of smallpox introduced earlier by white traders. By now there were a
mere 1000 left. At first they naïvely aided the colonists,
teaching them the techniques of growing corn. They
were unaware that as they helped, the Christian
Puritans were praising the Lord for the scourge that
had cleared out the savages.

Not all New England tribes welcomed the Europeans. The Pequots in particular had reason to resent
the English. While they had never attacked an English
settlement, they themselves were raided in 1636 by a
force of Puritans on the trumped-up charge of their
harboring the murderer of a drunken trader. The raid

was inconclusive. The Pequots were warlike and powerful, had conquered over 25 villages and posed a threat to English settlements. So the following year the English, allied with over 1000 Narragansets, waged a war of extermination, completely destroying the Pequot nation.

As the colonists prospered, so did their ambitions, hampered only by the presence of the Indians. By 1671 the proud Wampanoags, threatened by outright war, yielded to the English yoke. Metacom, their chief, agreed to pay a hundred pounds annual tribute. But Metacom, known as King Philip, was biding his time. By 1675 his diplomacy had won the great Narragansets to his side and war burst upon the surprised New England settlements like a blood bath in a slaughter-house. And the Puritans reacted in kind, butchering women and children, gloating in the riddance of the savage heathens. In the summer of 1676 King Philip was killed, his severed head displayed at Plymouth before the very eyes of his captive widow. Outnumbered, outgunned, their leaders gone, the Indians' resistance collapsed. The white man's policy of extermination had prevailed again.

Sometime, almost before the memory of men, groups of Iroquois-speaking peoples, kin to the southern Cherokee and Tuscarora, began moving north. Driving a wedge through the heartland of the Algonquian-speaking Shawnee and Susquahannas, the Delawares and Mohegans to the east and the Illinois, the Erie and the Miami to the west, the invading Iroquois established their villages in what is now New York State. Here they set up a sophisticated matrilineal government. Austere *sachems*, nominated by the female clan mothers, formed the ruling councils of the tribes. Under the imaginative statesmanship of one Hiawatha, not to be mistaken for the confused Longfellow's trumped-up and sanguine poetic protagonist, he helped form a league. Composed of the Seneca, Cayuga and Onondaga, the "Keepers of the Fire" to the west and the Oneida and Mohawks to the east, the Iroquois referred to themselves as the "Longhouse." The Senecas were known as "The Great Hill People," while the Mohawks were "The Keepers of the Eastern Door." With the arrival of the Tuscaroras from North Carolina in the eighteenth century, the Iroquois were known as the Six Nations and became the most potent political Indian force in Colonial America.

Their long, elm-bark-covered houses were set secure within stockades. Acres upon acres surrounded the villages. According to John Sullivan, the American general who ravaged their towns in 1779, he was amazed to observe the largest cornfields in North America.

The Iroquois, like many Indians, divided themselves into clans, the Bear, the Wolf, the Deer and so forth. Descent was reckoned through the mother's line and one's closest loyalties were to her family. In marriage, however, a spouse had to be sought from outside one's

clan and the new husband moved in with his wife's family. The women arranged the marriages, generally choosing a young man for an older, often widowed woman and conversely an older man for a younger girl.

This system had the great advantage of assuring the young people an experienced marriage partner. It obviated the risk of two young things wallowing in the mysteries of sex and marriage only to jeopardize the relationship. Furthermore, the young bride was assured the security of an experienced hunter who knew well how to provide, a successful warrior with status and position. The young groom, on the other hand, had the advantage of a partner who was wealthy in property, who owned the fields of corn, beans and squash and who was knowledgeable in the ways of parenthood and housekeeping.

The role of women in Iroquois society was indeed significant. Not only did the women arrange the marriages, own the utensils, the houses and the fields, but they alone decided who should be eligible for the positions of sachem. And their authority extended further; if a clan matriarch should disapprove of a sachem's actions, she could dispose of him forthwith.

Within the portrait:

MATOAKA ALS REBECKA FILIA POTENTISS PRINC POWHATANI IMP VIRGINIÆ

*Ætatis suæ 21. A°. 1616.*

Matoaks als Rebecka daughter to the mighty Prince
Powhatan Emperour of Attanoughkomouck als Virginia
converted and baptized in the Chriftian faith, and
Wife to the Wor.ll Mr Tho: Rolff.

**Left** Powhatan's cape. Chief of the Powhatans,
his daughter Pocahontas (**above**) was
christened and married an Englishman John
Rolfe. She went to London with her husband
and was received at the Court of Elizabeth I

The Iroquois men were the hunters and warriors and some became shamans and priests and council members. At the "Longhouse" the elders met to decide by unanimous vote civic matters as well as those related to making war or peace. In carving out living space in New York the Iroquois quite easily acquired numerous enemies. Their wars were ones of conquest and domination—the Hurons to the northwest were nearly annihilated in 1649, while the Delawares fell under the Iroquois yoke a little later. The Six Nations, jealous of the trading advantages of their neighbors, controlled the entire fur market by their military victories. During the French and Indian wars, while they remained more or less neutral, they did serve as a buffer for the British settlements against the French in Canada. During the American Revolution, with the exception of the Oneida and Tuscarora, they sided with the British. Under the leadership of Joseph Brant, the Iroquois ravaged the American settlements, burning, capturing, torturing and pillaging. Finally, incensed at the massacres, the Americans sent an army under John Sullivan which burned and totally destroyed all the Iroquois towns, an action which effectively broke forever the Indians' power.

Far to the south was the land of the Creek, the Choctaw and the Chickasaw. Here, in what is now Georgia, Alabama and Mississippi lived the descendants of the Temple Mound builders. To their northeast dwelt the Iroquois-speaking Cherokee.

**Right** A painting by John White showing the town of Secota with its typical Pamlico lodges and the figures dancing around posts
**Below** Among the Algonquians wampum belts were used as payment for services as well as a pledge **Far right** Red Jacket, a renowned Iroquois sachem

*Guerrier Iroquois.*

When De Soto invaded the Southeast in 1540 he observed the sacred Temple Mounds of the Creeks. This was a highly organized society which appointed from among its outstanding warriors a *mico* or king. So honored was he that he was carried around on a litter, his elaborately tattooed body the badge of his prowess in war. His council was composed of retired warriors, elders of recognized wisdom with whom he met daily. In a sense the Creeks were a confederacy composed of towns, first established in the northern part of their territory, later joined by other villages to the south. The original communities were known as "White" or "Peace" towns, the more recent ones were referred to as "Red" or "War" towns. It was from the Red town that the war chief was chosen—in reality a priest versed in the mysteries of successful battle.

Boys were early taught the skill and techniques of war, for this was the profession to which men aspired. War was waged for a variety of reasons, sometimes for conquest, sometimes to procure slaves, sometimes in retaliation for the loss of a beloved warrior. Indian attack was one of stealth and most often at dawn. Men were usually killed, women and children taken captive. Scalps were brought home to celebrate the victory.

War was a sternly cruel business and the Indians reveled in it.

But all was not war and desolation. There was the necessary work of hunting and farming, there were games, and there were ceremonies associated with marriage and the new crops and death. One of the favorite games was lacrosse. The players, often representatives of different towns, were supplied with little rackets. With these they tossed a small ball, endeavoring to hit the opposing team's goalpost set up at the opposite end of the field of play. There were no boundaries and few rules. A player might run for hundreds of yards or even miles eluding his opponents to achieve a great end play. Stakes, in the form of costumes, food, in fact all manner of possessions, were offered up. For Indians gambling was as much a part of a contest as was the game itself.

In the early summer, just as the first corn was ripe, the Creeks held a most impressive ceremony. This was the time of purification and renewal. People busied themselves sweeping the village paths, destroying old clothes, breaking up their clay pots and bowls and extinguishing all fires. A new fire was set in the plaza where the men for four days were harangued by their

**Left** St. Sauveur's picture of an Iroquois warrior about to scalp a victim **Above** Portrait of Joseph Brant, a leading Seneca sachem who fought against the Americans

**Above** An engraving by Hendrick showing a Mohawk sachem, his 39 victims displayed on a tree. The pipe-tomahawk became an important item of trade

J. Laroque Sculp.

Sauvage

leaders as they purified themselves with a powerful emetic. The whole affair was handsomely climaxed by a great celebration of feasting on the green corn, preening in new clothes, relighting the fires, and endless dancing with songs of rejoicing. And thus, the new year began, clean and fresh and joyous.

As was so often the case when the Indians first met the Europeans, they welcomed them. The Creeks did more than that. In 1732, in high hopes of obtaining great rewards in goods and education and the wisdom of the whites, several of their leading micos trekked for 25 days to meet with Georgia's governor. In exchange for little more than a conversation with James Ogle-thorpe, they literally gave him a sizable piece of their territory to start his new colony. At first, relations between the English and the Creeks were mutually profitable and Creek culture appeared to flourish. But as time passed unscrupulous traders, politicians, land

speculators and squatters had created such tensions, now within the Creek nation itself, that in 1812 actual civil war broke out. Taking full advantage of the conflict the then General Andrew Jackson used the old European ploy of arranging for Indians to fight Indians. With a force of militia, 600 Cherokees, Yuchi and allied Creeks, he utterly defeated the Creek dissidents and ended Creek power in the Southeast forever. Jackson became a national hero and his victory served as a springboard for his election as President.

Andrew Jackson, President, was a stiff-necked, pompous bigot. As an advocate of the white man's destiny he firmly believed the best Indian was a dead Indian. And with this conviction he rammed through, in 1830, the Indian Removal Act.

Very simply, this bill meant that eastern Indians would be forcibly evicted from their homelands and

**Pages 44-45, Left** A painting by F. Parsins of Cune Shote, a Cherokee. This headman wears two "Peace Medals" issued by the United States and a silver gorget, possibly given by the British
**Right and below right** An Iroquois warrior of 1787 by St. Sauveur. The carved wooden ball-headed war club could be thrown end over end to kill a man at 50 yards
**Left** A Choctaw Lacrosse game by George Catlin
**Below** Billy Bowlegs, a Seminole chief, from a painting by Charles Wimar **Bottom** A Seminole family in "chickee," dressed in traditional patchwork costumes

in turn given space in a newly carved-out piece of worthless country west of the Mississippi River, to be known as Indian Territory. Here the Indians might govern themselves, protected against land speculators, whiskey purveyors, unscrupulous traders. It was all very neat and tidy, somewhat like sending a naughty boy to boarding school and forgetting about him.

People from the Southeast, Cherokee, Choctaw, Chicasaw and Creek were physically removed from their homelands and militarily escorted to the Indian Territory in a trek which the Cherokee have sadly called "The Trail of Tears." But not all the Cherokees acquiesced; many hid in the vastness of the rugged Carolina mountains they loved. Nor did all the Creeks accept Jackson's fiat. The Seminoles, affiliates of the Creeks, escaped to the Florida everglades. After losing 1500 men in five years, the United States army finally gave up. The Seminole are still in Florida.

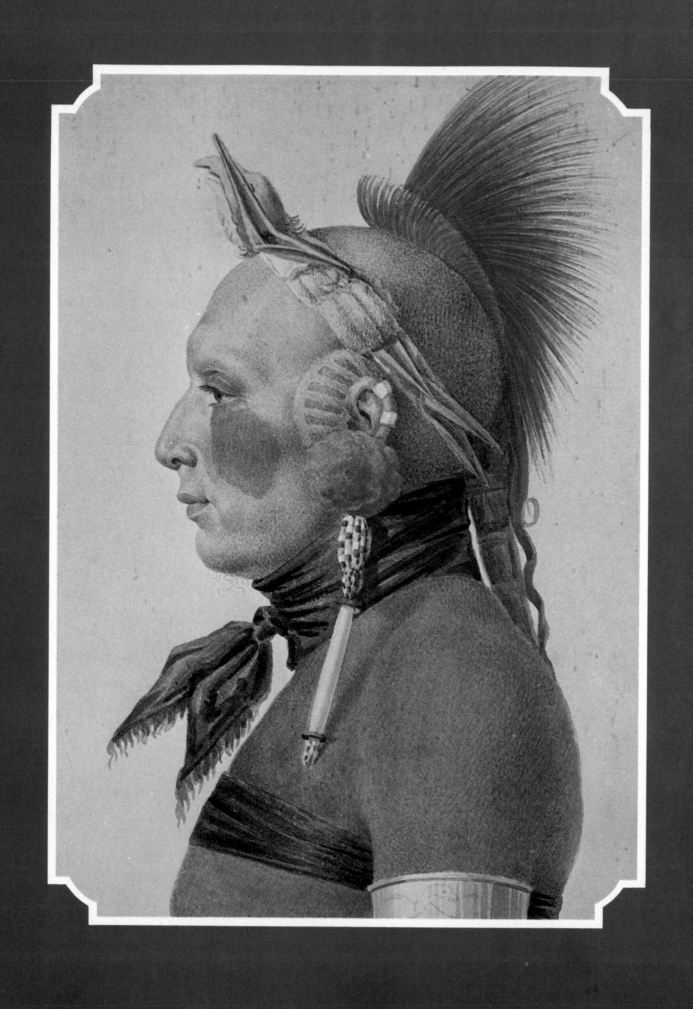

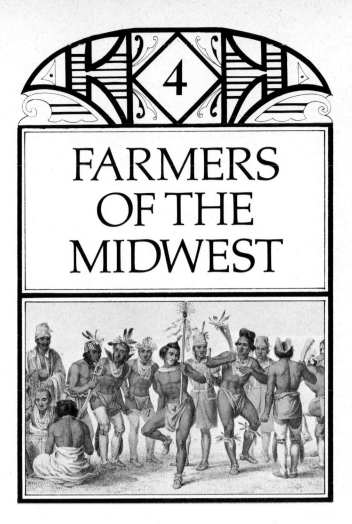

# 4

# FARMERS OF THE MIDWEST

**Left** An Osage warrior, painted by St. Memin in 1804 **Above** George Catlin's painting of an Oto chief. This man sat for his portrait in the 1830s **Above right** A war dance of the Sauk and Fox, usually performed in celebration of a victory; illustration from Mckenny and Hall

Close along the shores of the majestic and muddy Mississippi River just north of the great delta lived the elegant and highly sophisticated Natchez. Unlike the democracies of the Northeast, theirs was an autocratic theocracy of a most unusual nature. Their king or "Sun" was the absolute ruler of nine or more villages numbering over 4000 souls and was first encountered by the French in the late seventeenth century. So revered, so esteemed was the Sun that he was waited on by a retinue of dignitaries, carried in a litter from place to place, bedecked in a feather mantle and a plumed crown.

He resided on the plaza in an especially large house set atop a ten-foot-high mound. As chief priest his residence was close by the temple. This building, too, was placed on a mound, and while similar to his, was adorned with two carved eagles perched on the roof. Here the sacred fire was kept, together with the remains of former Suns. Only the Sun himself and specially appointed priests might tend the fire and guard the bones.

It was the Sun who appointed war chiefs, as well as other dignitaries, from among his relatives. They became known as Little Suns. The Sun might not, however, appoint his children to these positions. They fell into a social class below that of the Suns and became Nobles. The Sun's word was law, he received all the worldly necessities—food, drink, attire, even

*Plan du Fort.*

*Prisonier au Cadre.*

huge pearls for his adornment—as a kind of tribute from his people. He could command an army of workers or warriors at will and they served him without recompense.

The female Suns, likewise, held a phenomenally high and powerful position in the Natchez society. There appears to have been a principal matriarch and it was she who selected from among her brothers or sons the Great Sun. The social structure of the Natchez was complicated. Divided into several classes, the Suns were at the pinnacle. They were followed by the Nobles below whom were the Honored Men. Finally, at the lowest rung, were the commoners referred to as Stinkards. These poor people were considered as nothing more than mere scum, to be treated like dogs. In addition the society was divided along sexual lines with descent reckoned from the females. Thus the children of the female Suns were Suns, the children of female Nobles were Nobles, the children of female Honored Men were Honored Men. The offspring of Stinkards were obviously Stinkards. But the children of males, either Suns or Nobles or Honored Men, each dropped a class so that the child of a Sun became a Noble and so on. The Suns, whether men or women, could not intermarry. Strangely, everyone except the Stinkards had to choose a spouse from outside his class, and that class was the Stinkard!

What is so intriguing is that not only was such a genealogical system ever devised, but that records were kept without benefit of pen or paper.

**Above** The Natchez method of torturing an enemy, from a drawing by du Pratz c1718
**Below** The Great Sun of the Natchez is being carried to the Harvest Festival; also by du Pratz
**Right** Drawings of a Natchez temple and the dwelling-house of a Sun, the name given to the king of the Natchez

TEMPLE des Sauvages, construit de Poteaux en terre, revêtû de ... natte de canne, er couvert de même ... terminé par trois pi de bois, de 3. pieds ... de long 18. pouces et 4 po d'aïpaisseur, ... matachez et scu grossierement les ... 3. pyramides so natte garnie de ... canes pointû garentir, que ... son ne puisse monter au z ... figures qui rep -resente des ... d'Indes par corps et ... la queüe, la teste rep ... esente cell de l'Aigle ... ce qui nous parû de ... plus aprocha

me. Sauvage                    Sau va
                               ourson

CABANE du chef de poteaux en garnie de Bauge ou morr de terre, couverte aussy ... de natte, Le temple a 22. pieds de ... longueur er 12 pieds de lar il sert de sepulture au ... chefs de la Nations Toutes les Caban ... des Sauvages sont pareille Construct ... ion, etante toutes Rondes, celle cy ... a 18. pieds de diametre

Sauvage avec le Calumet          Jeunes Sauvag ou Bara

...vez et dessinez au Village des ... née. Redigez a la nouvelle Orleans le vingt et deux Juin 1732.

Throughout the Mississippi drainage area, both to the east and west, dwelt mound-building nations similar in many respects to the Natchez. Whether their social structures and kinship systems were as complicated is not really known. But such people as the Chitimacha, Biloxi and Alabama as well as the Atakapa, the Tunica and the great Caddo Confederacy, though often enemies, were agriculturists who were culturally quite similar.

To the north in what is now Missouri and Arkansas lived the Osage, Siouan-speaking farmers. A powerful and warlike group, their way of life was a reflection not only of aspects of southern traits, but also those of the eastern woodlands. Reminiscent of the South, their towns were divided between the factions of War and Peace. The War people ate only meat while the Peace people were vegetarians. On the other hand, their dwellings were patterned after those of the Powhatan, though here they were covered with hides as well as mats.

The Peace people chose a chief from among their elders or "Little Old Men" as did the War people. Each of the divisions was divided into several clans— the Elk and Pumas and Bear, the Deer and Crayfish and even the Thunder. The headmen of these clans were hereditary. Children were born into the clan of their mothers and were taught to respect their affiliation with deep loyalty.

Marriage was, to a degree, a matter of individual choice by the prospective partners, but the status, wealth and industry of the individual was a matter of concern and approval by the respective families. It was the young man who requested his relatives to make the overtures. Gifts were exchanged, the boy's family bringing horses, the girl's relatives offering clothing, utensils and sumptuous feasts.

The lodge, the clothing, the utensils, the gardens, even the children belonged to the wife. An Osage man lived, in fact, with his wife's family for whom he was expected to be a good provider. A considerate husband might decide to marry another woman, and as a matter of course be candidly asked to do so by his first wife. A second wife could help maintain the household and garden, but more important, she allowed the first wife time to enjoy the parties, the games like shinny and the vibrant meetings so vital to women. Younger sisters were most often chosen as a second wife in the knowledge that they got on better.

Osage women, like many Indians, were fastidious, bathing daily in the streams. After their bath the Osage anointed themselves with a perfume of columbine seed, calamus root and horsemint. Girls were most

A caddo village of thatched houses

often escorted to their baths by matrons simply because they were constantly subject to the gleeful spying of young boys.

At childbirth the women built a little hut for the expectant mother to which she retired. Here she was assisted by her mother and other female members of the family. The newborn was ceremonially bathed and given a name—a name like "The Wolf" or "The Small Beaver." Later, men might earn names from an important exploit, a typical example being "The Great War Chief." Nicknames were conferred because of a physical peculiarity, as implied by the name "The Lips," or as the result of a habit or style in battle as in "The-One-Who-Crawls-On-The-Ground."

Culturally the Osage, like many of their Siouan-speaking neighbors, the Oto and Missouri, the Kansa, the Omaha, Ponca, and the Quapaw were a combination of woodland farming peoples and prairie buffalo hunters. Before the advent of the horse the Osage hunters captured buffalo by surrounding them on foot. Men supplied with blankets formed a great V at the head of a gorge. While other men drove the herd of stampeding beasts toward and through the arms of the V, the men stationed along the wedge frantically waved their blankets. Yelling and hallooing, they frightened the onrushing buffalo toward the apex of the V and over the cliff. At the bottom, men with clubs beat to death those animals not already killed in the fall. Indians had been killing buffalo in this manner for thousands of years; it was quite an efficient method.

After the appearance of horses sometime during the eighteenth century, the Osage were quick to see the advantages of this animal. By increasing their mobility the hunters could more easily surround herds of buffalo they might not otherwise reach. Moreover, they could now be assured of an even greater kill. It was after the crops had been harvested and cached that the Osage left their villages for the fall hunt. Strict rules were made to guard against the buffalo being frightened away and police were appointed to enforce the rules. Overanxious individuals were prevented from hunting on their own lest the herd should escape. Even with the fleetest of horses surprise was essential.

If the Osage were successful hunters, they were even more noted as warriors. Their reputation was recognized, especially by the Pawnee and Comanche to the southwest. War parties, sometimes consisting of no more than five or six men, were organized by a war leader. Most Osage adventures seem to have been retaliatory in nature, such as revenge for a relative killed in battle. An enemy's scalp was evidence of recompense.

When captives were taken, mostly women and children, they were treated with kindness, sometimes as slaves, often as adopted members of the family. If, on the contrary, an enemy warrior's life was spared, he was brought home, tied to a stake and tortured by the women and young boys until he perished.

A successful war party returned in jubilance, but should a member have been killed, the war leader had to ask permission to enter the village. It was hoped that the relatives of the fallen warrior would accept restitution in some form of property, but if their anger and grief were great, the war leader might very well be killed. For the Osage war was a responsible business.

In the Great Lakes region of the Middle West were many tribes. Algonquian-speaking peoples like the Ojibwa, the Miami, the Sauk and Fox and the Illinois. To the northwest, Siouan speakers also inhabited the area—the Kickapoo and Menomini and the Winnebago. This was forest land and prairie rich in wild game—elk, deer, moose and bear. Even buffalo abounded, especially in the West.

The Sauk and Fox were a typical example of these hunting and farming tribes. Living in what is now southern Wisconsin, the Sauk and Fox had long been neighbors and were frequently thought of as one nation. They did, however, maintain their separate councils and, interestingly, their individual characters. The Sauk were recognized as straightforward and direct in their dealings, prosperous as farmers and

**Left** A delegation of Iowa and Sauk and Fox Indians in Washington **Above** Cheedobau, an Oto, holds an eagle-wing fan and brass pipe-tomahawk of European make

55

altogether an enlightened people. Not so the Fox. They seemed at odds with everyone. Warlike, indolent and greedy, they were not to be trusted and were accordingly feared, resented and thoroughly disliked. What kept such opposites together is a bit mysterious. Possibly it was a symbiotic relationship whereby the Fox profited from the Sauk's productivity, while the Sauk gained a powerful ally in war. They did, indeed, join forces to drive the Illinois from their territories and took for themselves the rich farmlands the Illinois had occupied.

As a woodlands people, the Sauk and Fox lived in bark-covered lodges, fashioned their canoes of bark as well as of logs. They placed their towns close to the waterways, for the rivers and streams were the Indian's highways. The women cultivated the usual crops along the fertile riverbanks in fields as large as several hundred acres. In the spring the maple trees were tapped for syrup. It was a land rich in wild fruits and berries and according to the famous Sauk leader, Black Hawk, they never went hungry for they always had plenty. During the fall hunt the Indians left their villages and traveled west in search of the buffalo and elk in the prairie country. Returning to their towns at the first sign of winter, they rekindled their fires to sit snug in their lodges till spring.

This was the time of year for storytelling, a time to recount the historical lore of the ancestors, the myths of the gods and supernatural beings.

The Sauk and Fox divided themselves into two separate divisions. Within each were several gens or clans given the names of their ancestors such as Bear or Sturgeon or Thunder and these became the totem of each family. Membership was by descent through the father's line and with it fell valuable property rights as well as important religious responsibilities.

The origin of the clans came through visions. Long ago when young men went alone to the wilderness seeking "power" from the supernatural, one man, for example, received instructions and rules of behavior from the Bear. These included the proper preparation of a bundle to contain items like the claw of a bear, the dried head of a special bird, and other objects considered sacred by the animal helper. If and when the instructions were adhered to precisely, the young man became possessed of superhuman qualities. Such might be the ability to foretell events, find lost objects and cure sickness by mysteriously causing the tent to shake violently as voices were heard and sparks shot about.

Bundles were handed down from father to son and the inheritor became the "Keeper of the Bundle," in a sense the priest head of the clan. The bundles were ceremonially opened during such auspicious occasions as spring planting and autumn harvest. At these times the clan members gathered to worship with song and dance, prayers and feasting, the proper delicacy being the flesh of a sacred albino dog.

Young boys were expected to seek a vision and some received sufficient power to become a shaman. Now he would be eligible to learn the feats of magic and to effect cures. At birth, boys were dubbed a color by their parents. Possibly the firstborn would be a black, the second white, and so forth. Throughout life they retained that designation for it served to show on which side one played in the ball games now called lacrosse.

The fate of the Midwest farmers after contact with the white men paralleled that of the eastern Indians. The Natchez at first were cooperative with the French. By 1722 the intruders had established plantations in the Indians' realm, built towns and a capital, New Orleans, in their domain. Inevitably, frictions occurred. A French sergeant shot an aged Natchez in the back in an argument over a debt. Men from the Natchez town of White Apple retaliated in kind. Angered, the French governor sent an expedition bent on destroying several of the Natchez towns, but when it reached them, the people had fled. The governor thereupon demanded the head of Old Hair, a town leader and, in fact, a Sun. And the war leader, Tattooed Serpent, brother of the Great Sun, acquiesced to keep the peace.

Matters, however, worsened, not only with the death of the Tattooed Serpent in 1725 and that of his brother, the Great Sun, in 1729, but with the arrival of a new French governor, who proved to be a most evil and rapacious tyrant. Demanding for his own plantation the young Great Sun's very town, he managed at last to exhaust the patience of the Indians. Enlisting the neighboring Choctaws as allies, the Natchez rose. Attacking the French settlement, they killed over 200 men and captured even more women and children. The governor himself was clubbed to death by a joyful Stinkard.

But the end for the Natchez was near. Their allies, the Choctaws, had tongues like snakes and sided with the French. This finished the Natchez and after only a few months of warfare, the Great Sun surrendered. Many escaped and sought refuge among the Chicasaws and Creeks, but the Great Sun and his family were sold into slavery at Santo Domingo. The French had got their way—the destruction of an Indian nation which had thwarted their imperialistic ambitions.

The fate of the more northerly tribes along the Mississippi and its tributaries, though by no means so quick and so final, was nevertheless one of anguish, cultural destruction and physical death. As early as 1804, land-hungry Americans were eyeing the fertile valleys of the Sauk and Fox. The United States' relentless expansion knew no bounds. Nor was there anything subtle about their determination. With audacious blatancy the American commissioners forced through an inequitable treaty under threat of military destruction. In fear and ignorance, the Sauk and Fox, as did so many tribes, naïvely signed away their lands and with them their very way of life.

Forced to move west of the Mississippi, one Sauk

group under the intrepid leadership of Black Hawk refused to accept the terms of the treaty. Instead, Black Hawk endeavored to enlist the aid of other tribes—the Osage, the Winnebago, the Cherokees and the Creeks. He and his son pleaded for their help to resist white encroachment. Skirmishes flared here and there and in 1832, with 500 warriors, Black Hawk and his band returned to their homelands. But his allies fell away and he attempted to surrender. Outraged when his peace emissaries were cold-bloodily shot down, he attacked the white forces with some success and retreated north. Here he was pursued by the militia and a party of Sioux. Cornered, he surrendered under a white flag, but his overture was ignored. Instead, his band was mercilessly slaughtered, men, women and children. Black Hawk escaped, only to be captured and imprisoned. Finally, in 1833, he was released to return to the forlorn remnants of his people in Iowa.

The Indian threat, the Indian obstacle to American destiny east of the Mississippi was shattered.

**Pages 56-57** The massacre of American prisoners which took place in January 1813. The British could not control the battle customs of their Indian allies
**Below** Black Hawk and his son, after a painting by John Jarvis

# 5

# WARRIORS
# OF
# THE PLAINS

High and barren, windswept and arid, the Great Plains are a hostile and foreboding region. In the north the winters are frigid, with howling blizzards piling snowdrifts in all the cuts and coulees. Summers on the southern plains are unbearably hot with dry winds searing the grasses and drying up the streams. Along the wide and shallow rivers which can become raging torrents from the flash floods of summer, are groves of cottonwood and box elders, chokecherries and wild plums. To the west along the high ridges are stands of ponderosa pine and cedar.

Once, huge herds of buffalo roamed by the millions up and down the unending sea of grass. Mule deer browsed in the wooded areas while antelope grazed the high, rolling ground. The black bear and grizzly rummaged everywhere in search of berries, fish and honey, while wolves and coyotes and fox grew fat from an abundance of jackrabbits and prairie dogs. Golden eagles soared in the high, blue sky, ducks and geese made their flyways above the land while prairie chickens strutted their strange mating dance in dusty circles on the flats. It was a big country, a rich country and the men who wrested a living from it had to be of hardy stuff. And the Indians of the Plains certainly measured up handsomely.

Among the earliest settlers in recent times to venture onto the Plains were pioneers from the East. Southward, it was the Caddoan-speaking Wichita who inched their villages west along the rivers. Here in grass-thatched beehivelike lodges, these farmers set their towns in what is now Kansas, Arkansas and Oklahoma. Some called themselves Kichai and Tawehash, Tawoconi and Waco. All were closely related, all lived in a land rich in buffalo, all were referred to as "Pawnee Picts" because of their custom of elaborate tattooing.

**Previous pages, Left** Counting Coup. The first man to strike or "count coup" on an enemy earned the most credits **Right** A participant in the Sun Dance; by Remington
**Below** A Pawnee earth lodge village on the Loup Fork, Nebraska **Right** Drawing of a Wichita village of grass lodges at the foot of the Wichita Mountains

Siouan-speaking people, the Omaha and Ponca spread west from the Mississippi valley to parts of Kansas, Nebraska and the Dakotas. Here they built great earth lodges, domelike structures of logs covered with sod. Outside the stockaded villages, the women tilled the fields.

The fact that the women were the farmers has somehow led to the mistaken belief that the Indian woman's status was inferior. Other factors, too, added to this misconception. It was the women who carried the burdens, the cradled infants, the loads of firewood. When the people moved, it was the women who followed behind the men in single file, an apparently subservient position. Polygamy, too, at first glance, suggests a male chauvinism. Indian men might marry from two to six or even more women, depending solely upon how many they could provide for and keep happy. And that included the children.

**Below left** Arikaras performing the Bear Ceremony. The men sing as they shake gourd rattles **Below right** The Ducks, participants in an Arikara ceremony

**Right** Interior of a Mandan lodge, also used to stable the horses **Below right** Catlin's painting of the Mandan Okipa ceremony, the acquiring of power through self-torture

Divorce, too, was easy. A man displeased with his wife often needed to do little more than go to the center of the village, beat on a drum and announce something to the effect, "I don't want her, you can have her, she's too fat for me!" And an outraged husband, learning of his wife's infidelity, was entitled to cut off summarily the end of her nose. Without a doubt, this act to some extent reduced her allure.

White men, observing these customs, were appalled at the seeming mistreatment and inferior role of women. Knowing nothing and caring less for Indian cultural patterns, they were indignant for all the wrong reasons. But then, there is no one more blind and overbearing than the self-righteous.

The women performed the backbreaking labor of farming in large measure because the men's responsibility was to provide meat from the hunt and protection from marauding enemies. The Indian village was an armed camp. Men slept with their weapons at their sides. Except during the deepest of blizzards, no night was safe from attack. More significantly, women were associated with the birth of newborns, not only humans, but the sprouting of seeds, the product of the Earth Mother, the very source of all man's sustenance and well-being.

In a great many Indian societies, war was for men the motivating factor of life. The consequence of a war-oriented pattern, however, was a reduction in the male population. If women were to find husbands, they must be shared. Indians seemed not to have indulged in spinsterhood. Polygamy was a forthright solution. That the women should carry the burdens, that she should follow behind her menfolk on the trail was only logical. Men led the way as scouts and guides. Armed with bow and arrow, it was the men who could ward off an unsuspected enemy and defend his women against an unexpected danger. Unless these people had been living in some kind of Amazonian society, any other arrangement would have been absurd.

Divorce was easy, but since property, in so many of the tribes, belonged exclusively to the women—the lodge, the utensils, the fields, even the children—a man

64

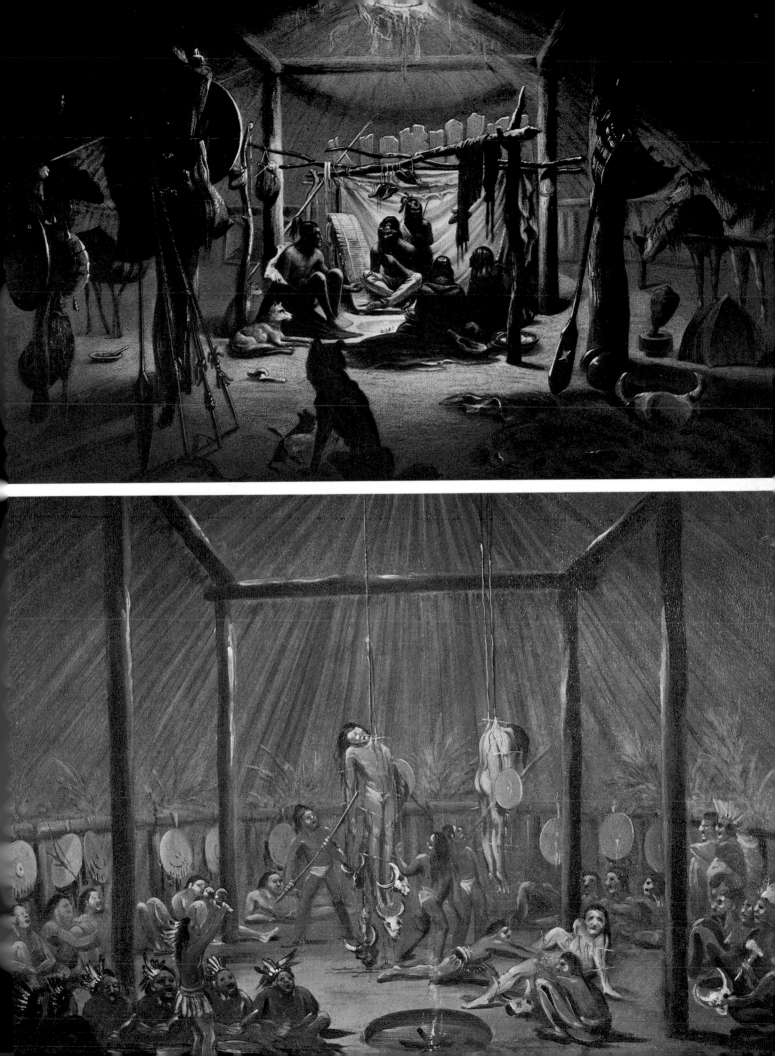

who was determined to divorce his wife had no place to go save back home to his mother. And about the only things he might take were the clothes on his back and his bow and arrow.

Disfiguring one's wife for an indiscretion was forthright, but a pretty risky business. In many tribes a man married into his wife's family. His go-between asked not only the girl's parents, but representatives of her family, in many instances her brothers. If the wife's family was a powerful one, mistreatment of one of its women could very well mean retaliation, sometimes in the stark form of murdering the husband.

The Indian family was of an extended nature and, depending on the tribe, traced its descent from either the female or male line. Matriarchs or patriarchs were the recognized heads of the family and as such were accorded respect and reverence. One married into his or her spouse's family and became part of that group. The idea of a man and wife setting out on their own as a conjugal family was not considered. The consanguine family wherein persons were related by blood rather than by marriage was the Indian pattern. The consanguine family has some interesting ramifications. In certain societies, children called not only their own

father "Father," but also their father's brother "Father." Conversely, they called their mother's sisters "Mother." And these tangential parents called these children "Son" or "Daughter." There were variations on this theme among the many tribes, but each possessed the principle wherein a child had several "fathers" and several "mothers." This worked in a very practical manner. In the event that a parent was lost because of divorce or death, the child was never the victim of a broken home. Rather he might still have several mothers and fathers who were responsible for him, for he was a member of a large and indestructible family.

One of the most westerly of the farmers of the Plains were the Pawnee. As earth-lodge dwellers, they set their villages along the rivers of what is now Nebraska. Here they grew crops in the summer, while in the fall they left their towns to hunt buffalo. The Pawnee were rich in ceremony and their most dramatic —the Sacrifice to the Morning Star—harked back to a far and ancient southern origin.

At the time of the summer solstice, just as the new corn began to sprout, a hereditary priest, keeper of the sacred bundle, now ceremonially opened it. Now, too,

**Left** An Arapaho medicine tepee displaying a quarter moon and a ceremonial calumet
**Below** Karl Bodmer's painting of a Mandan village on the Upper Missouri **Right** An engraving by Remington of a Plains Indian travois
**Overleaf, left** Three illustrations by Karl Bodmer. A Hidatsa dog dancer (**top**); a Mandan Indian (**center**); and Mandan dandies posing for the artist (**bottom**)
**Right** A Plains Indian encampment at the foot of the Rocky Mountains; painting by Bierstadt

Hidatsa dog dancer

Mandan Indian

Mandan dandies

a captive, a young maiden selected for the ceremony, was stripped of her clothing and her body symbolically painted. For several days she was accorded the greatest of deference and honor. But on the fourth day she was led to a platform where priests tied her and feigned to torture her. Then, just as the Morning Star rose, a warrior shot an arrow in her breast as another man at her back clubbed her to death on the head. Next, her heart was removed as a sacrifice to the Morning Star, whereupon all the men and boys filled her body with arrows. This was propitiation with a vengeance.

Early in the mid-nineteenth century, the practice was dramatically stopped. A young and respected warrior, indignant at the cruelty, dashed in on horseback, cut the binding thongs and rescued the victim. Rather than being punished, he was much honored for his bravery. The ceremony was discontinued and the Pawnee, surprisingly, actually seemed relieved.

The Mandan and Hidatsa living far up the Missouri River, like their neighbors, the Caddoan-speaking Arikara to the south, were earth-lodge dwellers. The Mandan and Hidatsa believed that the great, all-powerful "Wakanda," the Sun, imbued various animal emissaries with his power. Furthermore, if man was to be successful in his endeavors, he too must possess this power. Rapport with the animal agent, therefore, became essential.

For the Mandan, a more direct way of acquiring power was to undergo self-torture during the *Okipa* ceremony. Here men, under the direction of their mentor-priests, allowed wooden skewers to be thrust under the chest muscles. Thongs attached to the

**Above left** Crow men dressed in their finest regalia **Left** *The Man that Always Rides*, a painting by Paul Kane of a Blackfeet Indian. Upright bonnets were typical of the Blackfeet **Above** A Crow war party. The hooked lance or "coup stick" indicated officer rank

skewers were then drawn over the great log beams in the earth lodge. The participants were next pulled up so that they hung suspended several feet above the ground, all this amidst the singing of the spectators. With intermissions, when the performers were let down to rest, the ceremony lasted many hours to be concluded when the supplicants tore themselves loose. Painful as it was, the Okipa was the accepted way to communicate directly with Wakanda.

The Mandan, as did nearly all Indians, believed that the individual owed his existence to a thorough understanding and an ability to communicate with the world around him. Failure to comprehend the habits of the planets, the forces of nature, the customs of the animal nations, the desires and purgatives of the supernatural—the stars, the winds, the thunder and lightning, the causes of sickness—could each cause disaster and woe. The Indian believed himself to be an integral though infinitesimal part of the system of things. He did not command, rather he propitiated, gave offerings and thanks to nature for its every blessing. Through auspicious ceremony he tried to control nature, insuring its beneficence and allaying its wrath, all toward the end of existing within its demands and understanding its complexities, all for his own security and well-being. His aim was to draw power from the order of things, never to disrupt that order.

In the late eighteenth century, the Mandan were a prosperous people living in as many as thirteen stockaded villages with an estimated population of 3600. They split themselves into two parts, the "Lefts" and the "Rights" and these were in turn divided unequally into seven clans with inheritance reckoned through the mother. Representatives of each moiety and each clan could be found in all the villages. In marriage, one had to choose a partner outside his or her moiety as well as from a different clan.

The headmen or council of elders chose from among themselves one peace chief, one war chief and one civil, or village chief. Men achieved these positions by proving themselves good hunters and providers and by exhibiting prowess in war. But more important, they had to be recognized as possessors of exceptional power, not only by their successes, but by the aura of wisdom they displayed.

It was during meetings of the councils that the ceremonial smoking of the pipe took place. It was considered essential to preface important events, both civil and religious, with appropriate supplication to the gods, and the pipe was the instrument through which the smoke of tobacco would convey the Indian's appeal.

Among many tribes, the pipe was a badge of high office. "Pipe Owners" were invested with authority to lead the bands when moving camp, to select the new village site, and most important, to settle quarrels among men by offering the pipe of peace and goodwill.

Smoking was common throughout North America, and while pipes fashioned of stone and clay were predominant, cigarettes were used in the far Southwest. Both men and women smoked for pleasure and their pipes were unadorned, but the pipes reserved for ceremonial use were highly elaborate. Carved stems, sometimes three feet long, were decorated with porcupine-quill embroidery and the green neck feathers of mallard duck or a pendant fan of eagle feathers. The latter were referred to as "calumets" and were as reverently respected as any European monarch's scepter. The pipes, often in the shape of an inverted T or in the form of an animal or human effigy, were carved from red catlinite or black steatite and often inlaid with lead.

Young men worked hard to achieve status. On the battlefield they fought warily to strike the enemy and earn "coups," points toward their war record. Young men joined police and warrior societies, paying an initiation fee in goods. Some also took up the ways of the shamans and might become priests and the keepers of sacred bundles, keepers of the ancient lore and rituals of the Mandan.

Because the Mandans were light of complexion, possessed shorter and more aquiline noses than their neighbors, and because some of their women, even young girls, had silvery grey hair, it was long believed that they were in fact descendants of a lost Welsh

colony. The theory, of course, was absurd. The fact was that a strange lack of melanin was genetically transmuted to the female. The Mandan were no more Welsh than were the Indians throughout America descendants of the Lost Tribes of Israel.

Dogs for the Mandan, as was true for most tribes, were originally the only beast of burden. The Mandan villages were literally alive with them. It was not unusual for a family to own as many as 40 of man's best friend. During the fall hunt, dogs were harnessed to an A-shaped frame or *travois*. Here a leather harness was fitted over the shoulders at the apex as the arms dragged behind on the ground. A small platform of sticks, or sometimes a hoop latticed with rawhide much like an oval snowshoe, was lashed to the arms of the travois to support the load. On this platform were piled the *parfleches*, painted leather envelopes that

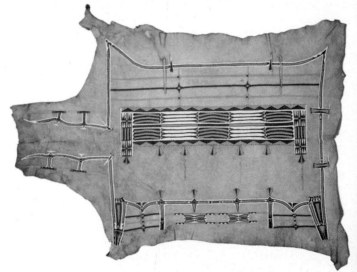

**Above** The Buffalo Hunt, a painting by Charles
Russell. A two-year-old cow was considered the
most desirable capture
**Far left** This beaded buffalo robe would have
been worn by a Sioux woman a century ago
**Left** Assiniboin Indians hunting on snowshoes:
from a painting by Peter Rindishbacker

served as suitcases, or the bundled tepee. Sometimes miniature domed cages made of willow rods were fashioned to become a tiny playpen for small children. In the winter, dogs pulled laden toboggans over the snow and icebound rivers as their masters, the women, drove them along.

Dogs were not only draft animals, they were an important part of Indian diet. Boiled puppy meat was a delicacy served at feasts. Dogs were treated quite harshly by their masters, beaten and screamed at for such misbehavior as stealing food. Indians were generally amazed at the white man's attitude toward dogs. As one man expressed it, "White men beat their children and pet their dogs, Indians beat their dogs and pet their children."

The northern village tribes, the Mandan and Hidatsa and the Arikaras, as well as their relatives to the south, the Pawnee, had relatively minor, if any, real conflicts with the whites. The Pawnee realized the power of the Americans and decided to join them militarily as scouts against their enemies. The Mandans may have perceived the American strength too, but were destroyed, and destroyed without a fight in a most insidious and tragic manner. Smallpox struck their villages in the late eighteenth century. Epidemic followed epidemic. When Lewis and Clark, the hardy explorers of the United States' new Louisiana Purchase, wintered at the Mandan villages in 1804, the Mandans reported that formerly they did not fear the Sioux, but that now their force of warriors was so decimated that they could barely defend themselves. Plague after plague fell upon them, cholera, measles, syphilis, tuberculosis, and always smallpox. And so, by the middle of the nineteenth century, there were a mere 39 ragged souls left in two dilapidated villages. In the case of the Mandans, there just wasn't any Indian barrier upon which the white man could vent his spleen.

The Mandan's sad demise in no way, however, spoiled the white man's churlish game of achieving his design to tame and own the West. The Americans continued to believe they had a God-given right to prove their destiny and that the best Indian was a dead one. While the sedentary village tribes wouldn't or couldn't muster much of a fight to disprove the white man's theories, the nomadic Indians of the Plains surely put them to the test.

From the Sioux, Cheyenne and Arapaho in the North to the Comanche and Kiowas farther South, these Indians fought to preserve their homelands with the ferocity of a cornered grizzly bear defending her cubs. The Blackfeet and Assiniboin and Crow to the northwest were so far removed from the main thrust of the white man's spearhead of expansion that at first they were affected only indirectly. The Sioux, on the other hand, situated in the very path of the Americans' drive, presented an exquisite example of a nation, a way of life, defending itself against imminent destruction.

As warlike, nomadic buffalo hunters, these tepee-dwelling horsemen of the High Plains came to symbolize all the heroism, drama and romance of the American Indian. Two factors, introduced by the Europeans, helped make for their brilliance—firearms and the horse. Driven from their original woodland home near the headwaters of the Mississippi by over-powering, gun-carrying Crees, the Sioux migrated to the Plains. Fortuitously, they acquired the horse sometime around 1740, but what was more, coincidentally they began to receive firearms and ammunition from American traders. Instantly the Sioux were invincible. They had the advantage over the Indians of the West who had no arms and over those of the East who had no horses. With this advantage, the Sioux held command of the heart of the northern buffalo range to become the masters of the Plains.

The role of men among the Sioux, as was true for all Plains tribes, was that of hunter and warrior. Hunting was an arduous task. The single hunter in search of deer must be wary, know how to stay off-wind of his quarry, how to shoot his arrow with uncanny accuracy. The Indian was a skillful bowman—he shot so powerfully that his arrow could completely penetrate a buffalo, he could hit his mark at 50 yards with absolute certainty and release his arrows in more rapid succession than a man could fire a six-shooter.

The communal hunt, as opposed to the individual hunter who sought his game on his own time, was highly organized. Scouts were sent out from the village to seek out the location of the herd. Once sighted, the men reported the appearance and numbers by riding their horses zigzag at the horizon, the distance they rode indicating the size of the herd.

Immediately, the police society assigned by the tribal executives or "Shirt Wearers," saw to it that no one started ahead lest the herd be frightened. Hunters who disobeyed this rule had their tepees slashed to pieces by the police.

When the signal was given by the leaders of the hunt, the riders pursued the stampeding buffalo. Seeking out a two-year-old cow whose meat was tender and whose hide the proper size and thickness for robes, the hunter rode close to the left side of the fleeing beast. Here he could shoot his arrow into the heart. Some men could kill from two to three animals in this way, others were completely unsuccessful. The rightful owner claimed his animal by the painted markings on the nock of his arrow as each man had his own mark. Those who did not make a kill were entitled to tie a knot in the tail of a fallen beast and thereby claim a hindquarter. Some men were "tail tiers" most of their lives, but to the competent hunter they offered an opportunity of being charitable and thereby gaining status for his generosity.

Young boys were taught the skills of hunting, war and horsemanship as early as the sixth year. To become a warrior was the ambition of every young man.

**Left** A Sioux girl wearing an elkskin dress with solid beaded yoke and a bone breastplate. She is holding a man's pipe bag **Right** A Sioux Indian woman with an Assiniboin child. The woman wears a painted robe and its designs symbolize the buffalo: an engraving by Karl Bodmer

As early as twelve years old, youths were taken on war parties as water boys, tending to the needs of the experienced warriors and watering the horses. The reasons for war among the Plains Indians were manifold—the defense of tribal territory or the expansion of it to secure better hunting, the capture of horses from an enemy tribe or retaliation for the death of a family member.

Horses were the basis of Sioux economy. With its appearance, the "Holy Dog" made the Sioux thoroughly mobile. Now they could hunt the buffalo much more effectively and over a much wider range. It was a well-known fact that the men with the fastest horses lived in the largest tepees. On horse-stealing expeditions, a skillful thief often tried to capture the enemy's fleetest horse—one that he might have observed on a previous war party. Horses were used as the standard of barter, shamans' families were paid in horses for effecting a cure, dreamers who made shields and war bonnets were paid in horses. Horses were given away to those who were owed gifts as well as to the needy. An individual's wealth rose with the number of horses he was able to accumulate, but he dare not keep them. His prestige and status were judged by the number he could give away. Owning property for property's sake was unthinkable; its sole value was that it could be shared with others.

A war party, often composed of no more than ten or twelve men, might combine both the purpose of horse stealing and vengeance for the death of a warrior. A man who had dreamed of the wolves—a shaman versed in the ways of war, who could foresee where the enemy camp lay, who could see around hills and ridges—was invited to join as war leader. The party might travel many days and cover several hundred miles. When close to enemy territory, the men traveled under the cover of darkness, resting unseen during the daytime in the protection of the wooded bottomlands. When at last they reached the proximity of the enemy village, they sought out a vantage point, sometimes as much as ten miles distant, to spy on the encampment. Here they might spend a day observing the village, drawing maps in the dust with a stick to plan the raid, watching the movements in the village, especially to learn where the horses were pastured at night.

Before dawn on the morning of the attack, the men prepared themselves for battle. They painted themselves in magic colors, marked zigzag lightning lines on their horses' legs to give them speed, partook of medicines to assure themselves power and gave some to their horses too. They dressed themselves in their finest clothes, for it was only fitting if one died on the battlefield that he be properly attired to enter the next world, "The Land of Many Tepees." Next they

This engraving by Karl Bodmer shows a Blackfeet warrior armed with a flintlock and musket, his bow and arrows carried in a quiver slung over his shoulder

*Wah-He-Jo-Tass-E-Neen*, an
Assiniboin chief, from a painting by
Paul Kane. His grizzly bear-claw
necklace was a sign of his bravery
*Hollow Horn Bear*, a chief of the Burnt
Thighs Sioux
*Fish Shows*, a Crow Indian
*Red Cloud* wearing a hair-fringed
shirt, the badge of an executive officer.
The locks, donated by a female
relative, represent the people of the
tribe for whom he was responsible
*Running Antelope*, shown to have been
a dignitary by the hair-fringed shirt
and the Peace Medal
*Four Horns*, an Arikara, typifies the
noble countenance of the Plains
Indians
*Two Moons*, a Crow headman

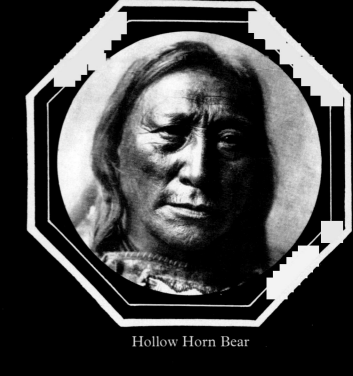

Hollow Horn Bear

Wah-He-Jo-Tass-E-Neen

Fish Shows

Red Cloud

Four Horns

Running Antelope

Two Moons

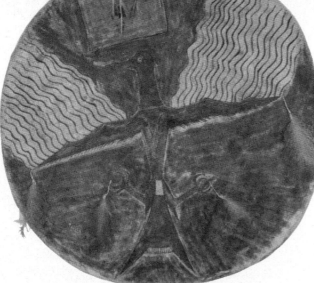

donned their painted buffalo-hide shields, painted by a shaman with magical protective devices received in visions from the supernatural. Those who had paid a shaman two horses for a war bonnet of golden eagle feathers put them on. The power of *Wakinyan*, the god of thunder and lightning, whose emissary was the eagle or thunderbird, protected one from the arrows of the enemy. When everyone was readied, the Wolf Dreamer, wearing a wolfskin over his head, performed special propitious ceremonies. The warriors walked their horses around hoping they would urinate so that they would be able to run faster. Then they sang their death song:

> *Now, tremble, O enemy tribe,*
> *I send forth a voice.*
> *Tremble, in a sacred manner,*
> *All sitting, tremble.*

Now, in the predawn darkness, they would leave

their hideout and stealthily ride toward the enemy's village. And at the moment of dawn, the warriors would charge, galloping headlong into the grazing pony herd, cutting them out and running them off, maybe as many as a 100 head.

It was customary for the Plains Indians to keep their prize horse—fast ponies with proven endurance—picketed close outside the owner's tepee. The enemy, alerted to the loss of their horse herd, were thereby quick and able to pursue the thieves on their fastest horses. Aware of this, the war party frequently split, the war leader assigning two or three men to hurry the horses toward home while the more experienced warriors would stay, not only to parry the enemy's attack, but also to do their best to collect scalps.

The opponents might now shoot at one another with arrows, but frequently the battle ended up in hand-to-hand fighting with lance and war club. The

**Left** A protective emblem painted on a warrior's shield by a Sioux shaman
**Above** Charles Russell's painting, *Jumped*. Emigrant trains on the Oregon and Bozeman Trails were prime targets for Indian raids

principal object was to strike the enemy, to count "coup" and thereby earn points for one's war record. Among the Sioux, the first to strike an adversary earned four points, the second three points, and so on. A man might kill an enemy with an arrow from a distance and receive no points as such, or a fifth man might kill and scalp a victim and be entitled to nothing. In practice, however, when one killed an enemy, the victor was entitled to paint a red hand on his shirt and on his horse, but a scalp was not reckoned in this system. It had another purpose.

A man who earned a first coup was entitled to wear a golden eagle feather upright at the back of his head. Men earning second, third and fourth coups wore feathers at different angles as badges of their bravery.

If the attackers were successful in repulsing the enemy, counting coup and taking scalps, they hastily withdrew in pursuit of their stolen horses. If the contest were close, they might well have lost one or two of their own. Since the thieves were usually out-numbered, their compatriots' bodies could rarely be retrieved. Rather they were left on the battlefield, left to the merciless scalping and mutilation by the enemy.

Upon reaching home, the warriors painted their faces black and rode into camp. If they had lost one of their party, four days of mourning was prescribed. Women wailed and the female relatives of a fallen warrior cut short their hair, slashed their arms and often cut off the first joint of their little finger. On the fourth day all grieving ceased, for now was the time for a victory dance, where the people celebrated, honoring in song and dance the exploits of the warriors. The scalps, tied on a stick, were given to the mother or sister of a fallen man with the accompanying statement, "Here is your son. Now his spirit may join his body. Now he will be permitted to enter the 'Land of Many Lodges.' Dance with this and rejoice for your son is now one."

The Indians believed that the hair continued to grow after death and was, in truth, akin to the spirit and with life everlasting. Hair cuttings and fingernail parings were secretly buried lest someone else find them and gain mastery of one's spirit. Throughout the Plains, scalping resulted in a vicious circle. Everyone was busy putting people together again. Any scalp would do; a woman's, even a child's served the purpose of re-uniting the spirits.

It has been said that the Europeans introduced scalping. This is not so. It is true that the French and English paid bounties which may have increased the practice, but that is all. Among Indians, the custom of scalping was based upon a philosophical concept surrounded with ceremony and deep-rooted tradition, none of which was so in Europe. Unlike an adversary's head presented on a platter to a king, the scalp was not a trophy, it was a symbol.

In order for a man to achieve true success in life, he had to seek a dream vision. Young men, under in-struction from a shaman, "went on the hill" for several days to fast and pray, smoking a pipe to propitiate the gods. The hope was that an emissary of *Wakan Tanka*, "The Great Holy," the Bear or Wolf, the Deer or the Thunder would give him instructions, rules and, above all, "power." Power was a force emanating from the gods which enabled men to achieve things beyond the capacity of ordinary mortals. Power enabled one to be a masterful hunter, to cure sickness, to foretell the future, to see around corners, to be invincible in battle. Instructions might include how to paint protective devices on shields or directions for the preparation of a medicine bundle. Rules might forbid an individual to eat certain foods lest misfortune befall him.

Men who had dreamed of the Bear were noted as specialists in curing, Wolf Dreamers specialized in warfare. Throughout the many bands, the dreamers formed themselves into little cults—the Elk Dreamers, the Deer Dreamers, and so forth. From time to time they performed before the people, testing their power against rival cults by spitting out grasshoppers adversaries had shot at them. The *heyokas*, dreamers of the Thunder, and whose specialty was finding lost articles, plunged their arms in scalding water un-harmed in order to impress the people with the power of their magic.

The epitome of the vision quest was the annual Sun Dance. Here as the bands gathered for the great summer council, men who had vowed to "dance gazing at the Sun" prepared themselves for the ordeal. Like the Mandan participants in the Okipa, the volunteers were suspended from a tall pole by thongs attached to skewers thrust through their chests. Gazing at the Sun, they danced several hours, finally to tear themselves loose. Those who completed the Sun Dance were entitled, after further instructions, to paint their hands red, a symbol of priesthood. Now they could officiate at important ceremonies, now they could speak in the secret tongue known only to the religious leaders.

Some young men, foreseeing the difficulties of the hunt and the dangers of warfare, the extremely rigorous and demanding life men must play, claimed to have dreamed that they were to assume the role of women. These transvestites, living together in tepees outside the regular camp circle, dressed as women and performed women's tasks—the tanning of hides and the embroidery with porcupine quills. Often they excelled the women themselves. The Plains Indian tolerated the homosexual, but upon death his spirit, like that of the murderer, remained in limbo, never entering the Land of Many Lodges.

The Plains Indians waged incessant warfare among themselves, and, with the encroachment of the white man, another enemy was added. Valiantly they fought to defend the lands. Kiowa and Comanche raided Texas settlements, continually pillaged caravans of freight and cargo along the Santa Fe Trail and even waged a pitched battle against the whites at the Adobe

Walls. The Sioux and Cheyenne long made travel on the Oregon and Bozeman trails hazardous. Angered at the construction of military forts on their lands, at the railroads cutting the buffalo ranges, the influx of miners scratching for gold in their sacred Black Hills, the Sioux retaliated. Sometimes with assaults on the wagon trains, other times with attacks on the United States Cavalry assigned to protect the trails, the Sioux, under the leadership of Red Cloud, waged war. Outraged, too, at the duplicity of the Washington commissioners who broke treaties before the ink was dry, at the unscrupulous traders rich with graft from short-changing on rations and rotgut whiskey, the Indians' attitude was anything but friendly. The United States, in its self-seeking omnipotence, not only forced treaties upon these Indians, but systematically killed off the buffalo. With the basis of their existence destroyed, the Indians were quite simply starved into submission.

Some Sioux leaders, like Sitting Bull and Crazy Horse, no longer able to endure seeing their people suffer the confinement and shoddy rations of the reservations, defied the government authorities and left. Now they could hunt in freedom. Early in the summer of 1876 a large encampment of Sioux, as well as some Cheyenne and Arapaho, ten to twelve thousand strong, had set their tepees along the west bank of Little Big Horn River in Montana. Sitting Bull, the highly respected headman and powerful shaman, reported having seen in a vision "many soldiers falling into camp." And within a very few days his prophecy came true.

In the early afternoon of 25 June, the Sioux in the Hunkpapa village at the north end of the great camp suddenly found themselves being attacked by a cavalry charged of some 140 "bluecoats." The Sioux were quick to respond. Warriors by the hundreds grabbed their weapons, donned their war bonnets and mounted their war ponies to repulse the invaders. And they were marvelously successful. Major Reno, whom the Indians did not know, and his troops were soundly beaten, the major leading a gallant retreat across the river and up the cliffs to a craterlike position which he hoped to defend. The much maligned Reno really had little choice. He was completely outnumbered and the promised support from his commander, the willful and arrogant General George Armstrong Custer, failed to materialize.

**Right** Sitting Bull holding a stone-headed war club and wearing a split-horn war bonnet of eagle feathers and ermine
**Overleaf** Two opposing views of Custer's Last Stand. William Dunton's painting of the Custer Battle is one of a number by white artists, many of whom never saw it **Inset** A representation of the battle by Kicking Bear, an Indian

W. Herbert Dunton.

No sooner had the Sioux spoiled Reno's plan—and he really didn't have much of a plan, his orders from Custer being simply, "Charge after them, you'll be supported by the whole outfit"— than the Sioux at the north end of the encampment saw troops. About three miles or more from the point of Reno's initial attack, the Indians observed cavalrymen riding along the ridge to the east. At first, a group of five or six valiant Sioux crossed the river hoping to stall the bluecoats' approach, hoping to protect the great camp, the women and children. They were being attacked by the dreaded *wasichu*, the child frightener, the "one who demands," the evil paleface quite properly nicknamed "Bossy."

Within minutes, not tens, not hundreds, but thousands of Indians came to the defense of the brave five or six defenders. More and more soldiers appeared along the ridge—215 of them, it is guessed—as Crazy Horse, Gall and others surged up the hill to surround

the scourges. And that is precisely what General Custer was. Authorized to help wipe out the Sioux recalcitrants, he undertook his job with glee. He also took matters into his own hands, foiling the planned pincer movement of General Terry's troops coming from the North and General Crook's advance from the South. Crook's forces, however, had been absolutely beaten by a Sioux force just eight days before at the Battle of the Rosebud. Crook returned to the safety of Goose Creek like a whipped dog with its tail between its legs. Crook never did show up.

Custer, in splitting his command, brilliantly failed in his promise to reinforce Reno. And poor Reno spent the rest of his life feebly defending himself as the scapegoat for Custer's impetuousness.

The Sioux, Cheyenne and Arapaho, outnumbering Custer's troops by as much as twenty to one, were quick to press their advantage. Black Medicine, or

mitted self-destruction hung forever in limbo, like those of murderers and hermaphrodites. Custer's body was found with a bullet hole in the chest and one in the temple.

It was a magnificent and symbolic victory for the Indians, but it was short-lived. In less than a year Crazy Horse and his 1100 followers surrendered. Sitting Bull escaped to Canada, but gave himself up in 1881. The power of the Sioux was crushed.

In 1890, having been inspired by the passive messiah Wovoka, a Paiute visionary, the Sioux, like other Plains tribes, embraced the "Ghost Dance" religion as a last hope. By strict adherence to the rituals and with the aid of the ancestors, it was believed the buffalo would return and the white men would just disappear. Government authorities, seeing the Indians assembled, grew uneasy and suspicious. Troops from the 7th Cavalry, Custer's old command, surrounded a group of Sioux with rapid-firing cannons. Arguments ensued and a shot was fired. Immediately, the cavalrymen commenced a barrage. Sioux men, women and children fought, some with guns, some with knives, some barehanded. Before it all ended, 29 soldiers were killed. Except for a few who may have escaped, all the Sioux perished. Custer had been vindicated at this massacre at Wounded Knee.

**Left** The notorious massacre at Wounded Knee, after a drawing by Mary Irvin Wright, 1896
**Below** By filling their enemies' bodies with arrows the Indians believed that the spirits of their dead victims could do no harm to the living: an engraving by Frederic Remington

Coffee, a nephew of Crazy Horse, having been wounded in the knee in the Battle of the Rosebud, rode up to observe the fight. "It wasn't much to see. Too much smoke and dust. It all ended about the time it takes a man to smoke a pipe." When it was over, when the last man of Custer's troops had been killed, the Sioux harassed Reno's stronghold and they would have destroyed him save for Sitting Bull's forebearing "There has been enough of killing."

The Indians scalped most of Custer's soldiers, stripping them of their uniforms, the women mutilating their bodies to prevent their spirits from haunting the world. Custer, also nicknamed "Long Hair" by the Indians, had had a haircut in accordance with army regulations just before the campaign. His body was found stripped but unmolested, and his scalp was not taken. To the Sioux, the scalp of a suicide was useless, for the spirit of those who com-

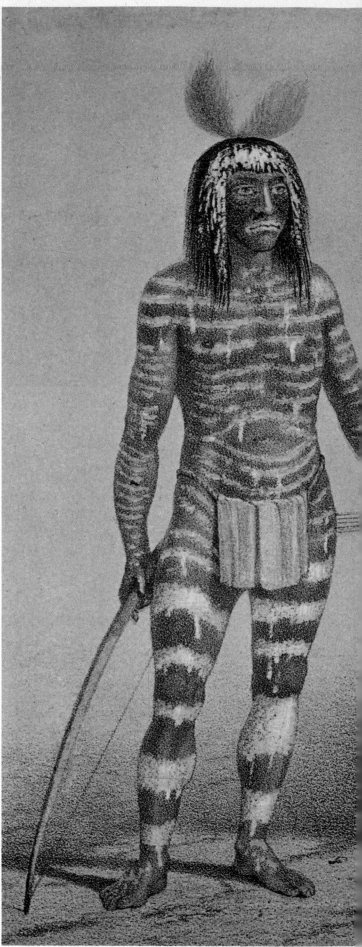

# 6

# GATHERERS OF THE FAR WEST

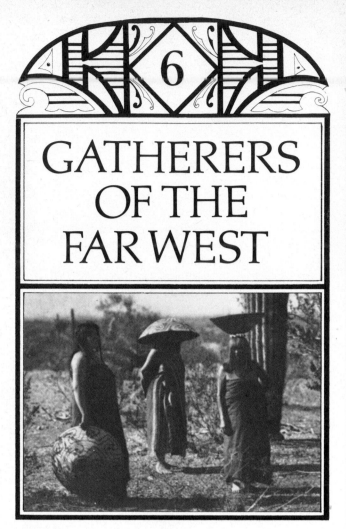

Nowhere was the struggle for life harder than in the Great Basin region of the West. It was a vast area including what is now western Colorado and Wyoming, parts of Arizona and most of Nevada and Utah. It was a parched and desolate country and places like Death Valley and the Great Salt Lake attest to the barrenness of this cruel desert. And it was here that the most primitive of all Indians lived.

People like the Paiutes and Western Shoshoni best typify the simple life of these poor Indians. The women devoted their lives to gathering seeds and berries in great baskets and digging for roots with sticks. White men, first seeing these Indians, dubbed them "Diggers." So disdainful were they of these primitive folk that when there was nothing better to do they organized hunting parties to kill Indians for fun.

Food resources were scarce. While some deer and antelope were present, rabbits and grasshoppers seemed to have been the staple. Rabbits were often snared in huge nets, while to catch grasshoppers, a long trench was dug several feet deep. The insects

**Above** Yuma women of the Southwest gathering the fruit of the giant Saguaro cactus
**Right** Striking Indians of the Southwest's Mohave Desert, underdressed and overpainted

**Left** Women of the Paiute tribe who had to cope in very harsh and primitive conditions
**Below** Paiute men. Indian men rarely had enough facial hair to grow beards
**Below Right** Arizona Paiutes on a seed gathering forage

**Overleaf** A painting by C. C. Nahl of the signing of the treaty with the southern Shoshoni. Treaties of this kind were invariably broken, never by the Indians, always by the white man

were then flushed and driven along until they hopped into the trench. Here they were roasted alive. According to these people they made excellent flour. Lizards and caterpillars were delicacies and rats were good too.

The Indians lived in little wickiups of sticks and brush, always moving their tiny camps in an unending search for food. Their clothing was scant. Men wore only a breechcloth, if that much, while the women wore short fore-and-aft aprons of cedar bark and a basket hat. Both sexes wore sandals and in winter rabbit-skin robes were common.

There was no government as such, but when decisions needed to be made with respect to a hunt, an elder might be appointed to be a "talker." With regard to marriage, a man might have two wives, but if there was a shortage of women, a wife might have two husbands. When someone died, the hut was burned and the name of the deceased never spoken lest the voice of the dead return.

Like the Pueblos of the Southwest, these were a peaceful people, fighting only to defend themselves. Isolated and moving in such small groups, they were rarely bothered by enemies. They were hard to find and really had nothing anyone wanted.

**Left** A Havasupai dwelling. The Havasupai were considered a gentle people **Above** A Papago grass house in the Arizona desert

In the valley shelves of the Grand Canyon of Arizona, the Havasupai hid, protected by the massive walls of rock. Their way of life was similar to that of the Basin peoples, but like their naked neighbors, the Mohave farther down the Colorado River, they had little gardens and raised crops. Their greatest claim to fame seems to lie in their renown for a polite consideration for others. For example, the Havasupai had a particular concern, when twins were born, about determining which of the two was the elder. This was easily resolved, however, in the knowledge that the older, in deference to the younger, would stand aside just prior to birth, allowing the second born to come into the world first. Hence the last born was obviously the elder. The Havasupai are rarities among men for they are a truly gentle people.

North of the Great Basin was the Plateau region, somewhat less inhospitable than the Basin, yet still anything but lush. This was the country of the Flatheads and Bannocks, the Coeur d'Alene and Nez Percé. Here the hunting was better. Deer, elk and mountain sheep were plentiful in some areas. Fish, especially salmon, were abundant along the Snake and Columbia rivers during the spring season. When smoked, large quantities could be preserved. The women, like the Paiutes, gathered berries and wild plants and dug for bulbs and roots. They, too, wore aprons and basket hats which later they embellished with beads. In the winter the people wore robes of rabbit skins and sought shelter in pit houses covered with brush or mats. While life was better than in the Basin, it was hardly luxurious for the Indians of the Plateau.

Seeking visions was highly important to these people, for only through this quest could one obtain a guardian spirit. Both boys and girls sought this gift, but young men were much more determined. All manner of trials were endured; scratching oneself with thorns, diving into icy water and fasting at a lonely vigil

**Above** A Washo basket made by the master craftswoman, Dotsolalee **Right** Pomo feathered baskets were ornamented with shell beads **Far right** A Papago basketmaker **Below** A Pima Indian village painted by John R. Bartlett **Opposite** Big Knife, a Flathead, wears an ermine bonnet with split horns and he carries an eagle-wing fan

were commonplace. It was only later in life, however, that the spirit informed the individual of his blessing.

Some men became shamans endowed with the power to cure. Sickness was caused by worms or sticks entering the body or sometimes by the loss of one's soul. Medicine men were skillful in sucking out the foreign matter with tubes as well as in recapturing a lost soul.

The Utes, whose territory embraced what is now western Colorado and southeastern Utah, formerly lived much as their western relatives, the Paiutes. Theirs was the rugged mountain country of the Rockies. But for an amazing event, they might well have remained a simple hunting and gathering people, poor and struggling.

Sometime around 1650, the horse appeared. Strays from Coronado's legions and later from Spanish rancheros formed herds of wild mustangs. It was possibly these the Utes first saw or they may have obtained them from Apaches and Comanches who had got them earlier. In any event, with the introduction of the horse the Utes' whole life-style blossomed. Mounted on horseback, they became fearsome marauders. They could leave their mountain fastness and successfully hunt the buffalo on the plains below.

At a later date, the Shoshonis of Wyoming obtained horses. They, too, now hunted in the grasslands of the Rockies' eastern slopes. The Umatilla received horses in the late 1730s, as did most of the Plateau people. With this advantage their lot improved. Many of the little tribes assumed the attributes of the Plains

**Left** A Pima matron and **Right** A Southwestern girl of the Maricopa tribe. Women from this region were renowned for their beautifully fashioned and much coveted baskets

Indians in costume, hunting techniques, even to adopting the tepee. One group, the Palouse, became somewhat adept at horse raising and from their reputation derives the breed of horses known as Appaloosa.

The lands of the northern Plateau Indians lay directly in the path of American expansion. In the mid-nineteenth century pioneers sought new lives in the Oregon Territory, miners grubbed and dug and panned for quick riches in gold and the United States Cavalry were ever present to protect the interests of these white intruders. Treaties were made in which the Indians relinquished their lands. These were repeatedly broken, never by the Indians, always by the whites.

In 1877 Chief Joseph, of the Nez Percé, refused to renegotiate the terms of the unconscionable treaty of 1863. Moreover, he withdrew, firmly convinced

justice would not be done. Taking many members of his tribe, Joseph led a masterful retreat north toward Canada, outmaneuvering and outfighting the pursuing troops. At the Yellowstone River in Montana, however, he miscalculated and was cornered by General Miles. Here he surrendered and was promptly imprisoned at Fort Leavenworth, Kansas. Later released, Chief Joseph returned to his people. He had earned not only their love, but the respect of the United States' military leaders as one of America's outstanding strategists.

As with all Indians, the Plateau people regretfully ceded their lands. That sorrow was eloquently expressed to the governor of Wyoming by Chief Washaki of the Shoshonis in the oratory for which American Indians were so famous. (Part of the text of this moving speech appears on page 103.)

California, before the coming of the Spaniards, was

a medley of colorful little tribes. They occupied themselves in hunting small game, gathering acorns and wild vegetables, making exquisite baskets and celebrating life with elaborate ceremonies. In this fabulous region were representatives of nearly every linguistic stock found in North America. Everybody seemed to like to go to California.

Acorns were the staple, but removing the bitter tannic acid from the nuts required cracking them, grinding them several times, leaching and roasting the nuts in order to make a palatable flour. This was the work of the women. In addition to their ingenuity in food preparation, the women fashioned baskets of superb beauty, unrivaled throughout America.

They made huge baskets for holding mush, four feet and more in diameter. They wove baskets as tiny as a pinhead with stitches so fine that they can be counted only under a magnifying glass. Some baskets were coated with ugly pitch to make them watertight, others were interwoven with brilliant feathers and suspended shells to create veritable jewels of artistry.

As hunters and warriors, the men were equally clever. In hunting waterfowl, for example, men would float large gourds downstream past a flock of sitting ducks. When the birds became accustomed to the presence of the strange objects, the hunter would place a gourd over his own head and submerge himself in the water. When close to a duck, he would grab the bird by the feet, pull it under and drown it. A careful hunter could collect quite a few birds using this trick. Another stratagem the hunters figured out was that by using a reed straw through which to breathe, a man could sink below the surface, approach the waterfowl and pull under as many birds as he could manage to hold in his hands.

The Californians were a very belligerent people,

**Above left** Chief Ouray of the Utes. With the introduction of the horse the Utes becáme successful buffalo hunters **Left** California Indians dance before the Mission at San Francisco **Above** A woman of the Nez Percé tribe wearing a beaded yoked dress and a basket hat **Right** A painting by Paul Kane of a Nez Percé near the Columbia River **Far right** Another painting by Paul Kane shows Caw-Wacham, a Flathead woman. This kind of head deformation was achieved by means of a cradle board

iaus in the Lava Beds,
aliferia. April 187

assiduously guarding their territories, and repulsing trespassers with vigor. Miniature wars broke out continuously, mostly over disputes about their borders. On occasion, to settle matters, the opponents chose two of their most able warriors who then battled among themselves. The group whose man was victorious decided and settled the issue.

The Californians had two overriding interests: money and death. They acquired and carefully accumulated shells: clam shells cut to the size of a thumbnail and dentalium. The latter was a white, curved, cone-shaped shell and its value depended on its length. Shells were used for the payment of all obligations as well as for trade. So widespread was their worth that the well-to-do Sioux women of the Plains bartered for them to decorate the yokes of their dresses, thereby displaying their wealth. This, parenthetically, typifies only one of the many complex trade routes the Indians had developed throughout all the continent.

Among most California tribes, death prescribed elaborate ceremonies. The Californians divided them-selves into moieties or opposites. On this sad occasion, relatives of the deceased sent emissaries to the opposite branch. Bearing shell money, the bereaved requested members of the other moiety to officiate at the funeral lest the family, by being in too close contact with the dead, might be adversely affected. At the funeral, the house was burned, the body cremated and the name of the deceased never spoken again.

At the end of a year more death ceremonies were held. Myths about the Eagle, one of the first ancestors, and his untiring search for life only to find death, were recounted in great detail. The Californians had fun celebrating in morbidity.

The demise of the Californians was the same sad story as elsewhere throughout the nation. What the Franciscans and their missions didn't destroy psychologically, the settlers and miners did physically. The Indians were in the way. By 1850, it is estimated that there were barely 17,000 Indian survivors in California from a once rather thriving population of some 200,000 in 1800.

*The white man's government promised that if we, the Shoshonis, would be content with the little patch allowed us, it would keep us well supplied with everything necessary to comfortable living, and would see that no white man should cross our borders for our game, or for anything that is ours. But it has not kept its word!°*

*The white man kills our game, captures our furs and sometimes feeds his herds upon our meadows. And your great and mighty government . . . does not protect us in our rights. It leaves us without implements for harvesting our crops, without breeding animals better than ours, without the food we still lack . . . without the many comforts we cannot produce, without the schools we so much need for our children.*

*I again say, the government does not keep its word. And so, after all we can get by cultivating the land, and by hunting and fishing, we are sometimes nearly starved, and go half-naked, as you see us! Knowing all this, do you wonder, sir, that we have fits of desperation and think to be avenged?*

**Above** The text of the now famous speech delivered by Chief Washaki of the Shoshonis to the governor of Wyoming expressing sorrow at the white man's inability to "keep his word" **Right** Chief Washaki himself **Left** The California Modocs' last stand in April 1873: a watercolor by William Simpson

**Above** Drawings by
Alexander Malaspino of a
Northwest Coast warrior
in slat armor and with his
grotesque mask
**Right** A Northwest Coast
village—possibly Haida—
photographed in the 1880s

# 7
# SEAFARERS OF THE NORTHWEST COAST

The coasts of Alaska and British Columbia are a humid, narrow strip of pine-and-spruce-covered shorelines faced by the Pacific to the west and backed abruptly by mountains to the east. Deep blue rivers flowing through mighty fjords abound in salmon. Bear and deer and mountain goats were common and the ever-present raven frequented the dense forests. Whales, porpoises and seals roamed the coastal waters. And with this natural wealth, the Indians who lived there themselves became fabulously rich. Men like the Nootka and Haida, the Tlingit and the Tsimshian set their villages along the beaches, close to the source of their livelihood.

These were a warlike people, their wealth and consequent overpopulation helped to make them so. Valuable fishing sites were coveted and defended. Warriors wore armor of wooden slats and great carved wooden helmets. Some of these were fashioned as hugely grotesque faces, which struck awe into the

enemy. When captives were taken they were kept as slaves to do housework for the upper class.

Each of the many villages had its own chief, who generally inherited his position from his mother's clan. With this position went many rights and privileges. Fishing grounds, for example, belonged to the chief and among the Nootka, the renowned whalers of the Northwest Coast, it was the chief himself who threw the harpoon.

Status and wealth for these people were of paramount importance. They decorated their housefronts with monstrous paintings of their clan ancestors—the Bear, the Beaver, the Raven or perhaps the Whale. Before their planked houses they erected giant poles embellished with their family crests. Totem poles were, in fact, a genealogical record of the owner's family and advertised to all his position in the community. Nearly everything they used, carved mountain sheep horn ladles, bentwood boxes, canoes, even the paddles were decorated with stylized representations of the mythical animal ancestors.

Aesthetically, the art of the Northwest Coast was the most elaborate and highly sophisticated of any in North America. As carvers, the men were unsurpassed. From the massive forms on the towering totem poles and grave markers to the delicate openwork on the carved handles of their little, black mountain goat horn spoons, the workmanship was masterful. Bowls were carved from a single log and decorated with incised clan motifs. These were painted in red and black and embellished with inlaid shells. Some were effigies in the form of a frog or bear, others, almost life-size and portraying a man on his back, were used in the great feasts and the ceremonial give-aways called *Potlatches*.

The art of the Northwest Coast was varied. Some was strikingly realistic as in the portrayal of the human face in certain of the dance masks. Most of it, however, was intricately stylized. Representations of animals became designs, the subject often being split down the back to form a right and left. The figure became recognizable only by familiar marks—the beaver, for example, by his flat tail and immense incisor teeth.

While the men did carving, including the graceful canoes that might be as much as 50 feet in length, the women wove baskets of superior quality. They made capes and wraparound skirts woven of shredded cedar bark. They also fashioned wide, conical basket hats whose design was perfect for shedding water in the rainy climate of the Northwest. The women at Chilkat wove blankets of mountain goat and puppy dog's hair, displaying the owner's crest in cryptic designs with muted yellows and blues outlined in black.

As is true for the majority of American Indians, the art forms of the Northwest Coast people were developed as embellishments to functional items. Even the totem poles exhibit this principle, for aesthetically handsome as they may appear, their purpose was strictly one of displaying the owner's social position. The relatively recent concept of art for art's sake was unthought of by the Indian, and yet by harmoniously combining color with form to create a pleasing balance in the objects they designed for practical use, they achieved a work of art. Almost as if innately, through

**Below** Skidegate, Queen Charlotte Island, British Columbia **Above** An Alaskan chief's house. Housefronts were frequently decorated with stylized representations of the occupant's mythical animal ancestors

generations of experience, uncounted years of trial and error, the object turned out perfectly. Here was an artistic accomplishment that was not only remarkable in itself, but indisputable in its individuality.

Unlike European art which to be good must be pleasing or striking to the eye, to be acceptable to the Indian, it must be correct. The Indian artist worked within rather rigid bounds determined in large part by natural resources and traditions. While, it is true, a variety of colors were found in certain areas in the form of plant dyes and earth colors, the most universally available colors were red ocher and black derived from charcoal. And this combination is found again and again in the earliest collected specimens of Indian art. Limitations, too, were imposed upon the craftsmen by cultural traditions. There was the proper way to carve a mask, the correct way to weave a blanket. Consequently, the forms and designs were often so distinctive that in most instances tribal identification was readily discernible. And yet with all this seeming rigidity and conformity to tribal patterns, the Indian artist was careful not to repeat, not to duplicate a finished product. Hence, no two rattles were identical, no two decorated boxes were the same. Each, on the contrary, was an expression of the individual craftsman. And it is this principle that renders the art of the American Indians so enchantingly mysterious.

While wealth and status for the Indians of the Northwest Coast were in large measure inherited, maintaining one's high position required considerable acumen and a forthright show of power. War, of course, was one method by which a strong leader could prove his strength, but he needed also to be versatile in carrying out the Potlatch. This was the formal give-away ostensibly performed to display one's wealth and generosity, but actually to exhibit one's political clout.

The Potlatch was generally planned a year in advance, the clan chief directing his family, quite conceivably an entire village, to prepare not only enormous quantities of food, but a huge supply of blankets, boxes and all manner of useful and valuable items. When this mass of material had been accumulated, the chief would invite the headman of a rival clan and his people to the feast. Here, with everyone dressed in their finery, the host would distribute gifts to his guests—dozens of blankets and boxes and other articles he and his clan members had gathered together throughout the year. A sumptuous feast was presented with more than anyone could eat. To climax the Potlatch, the host might take one or more of his shield-shaped coppers, valued at perhaps 100 blankets, and hurl them into the sea. The host herewith displayed to the assembled throng his utter disdain for material wealth. This ostentatious exhibition was

For the Indians of the Northwest Coast social
position and wealth were of paramount
importance and these principles were embodied
in their art, as in the stylized totemic house post
(**above left**) and the painted housefronts and
totem poles (**above**) which detail the occupant's
genealogy **Left** Two boatloads of Kwakiutl
wedding guests

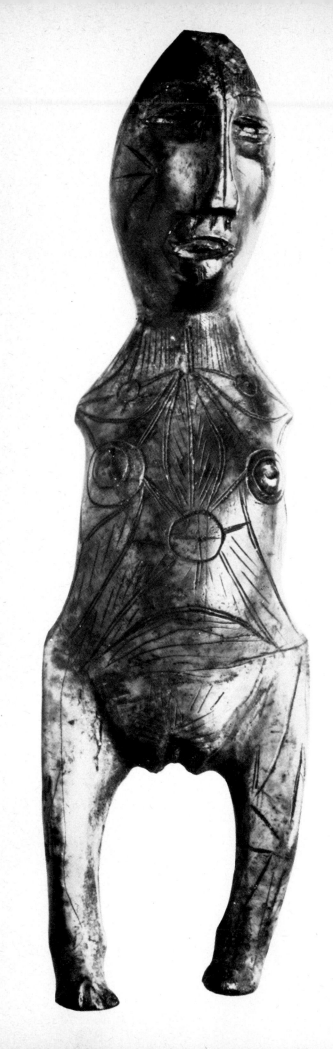

Far left Ovick ivory figurine from the Old
Bering Sea culture, c 300 B.C. Such figures are
thought to have been associated with fertility
rites Left A painting by Paul Kane showing a
Babine chief wearing a Chilkat blanket
Above Interior of a Nootka house, after a
painting by John Webber Below A Kwakiutl
Potlach feast bowl in the form of a sea otter

frequently accompanied by the killing of one or more
slaves, for as property, they now meant nothing at all
to their owner. It was a glorious occasion, a time for
receiving gifts, of feasting, of being honored by a
powerful and beneficent leader.

There was one catch, however, to the Potlatch. The
guest chief knew that within the year, all the things he
had been so generously given, all the display and
destruction of property, must be reciprocated, and
reciprocated with lavish interest. The Potlatch was, in
fact, insidious economic warfare waged with the
calculated design of ruining one's rival. And it worked.
Some headmen went bankrupt, others went mad and
not a few ventured upon suicidal expeditions of war.

Among the upper-class Northwest Coast families,
many of the rites and prerogatives and much of the
wealth were inherited. Even so, those so blessed did
best to seek visions. This was partly to secure those
benefits through supernatural aid, partly to obtain
membership in the secret societies. Magical ceremonies
were performed by such societies as the Bears and the
Cannibals. Masked dancers would impersonate the

mythical ancestors in the eerie shadows of the great planked houses. Phantom figures soared down from the smoke hole, some wearing huge beaked masks, opened by hidden strings, which clapped and banged, all to complete the ancient drama of man's mysterious past and to give meaning to his present.

Life among the Northwest Coast Indians was far from being a simple one. It demanded of the leaders vicious economic competition, a storehouse of memorized knowledge about the myths and traditions, rites and ceremonies which were essential to maintaining a cohesive and progressive society. It required physical fortitude in the hunt and in war, combined with an insight akin to wisdom as an arbiter in settling disputes. And finally, it called for that sense of leadership, that charisma that on the one hand brings loyalty and respect and on the other shows benevolence and understanding. Nor was life on the lowest rung one of mere simple servitude. In addition to the menial and often arduous work, the knowledge of having been captured as a slave could be pretty frightening. To

This chief's daughter is shown (**left**) painting a totemic design on a cedar bark hat and (**below**) wearing the same hat

realize you might well be killed to satisfy the economic ambitions of a copper-hungry chieftain displaying his disregard for wealth at your expense hardly equates with the simple, happy life of the noble savage.

No matter how rich in tangible objects, in ceremony and religion, in the products and resources of the fields and forests, in ideas of family arrangements and systems of government some native cultures might have been, or how poverty-stricken others seemed, the individuals worked hard to achieve their way of life and fought desperately to protect it. Throughout North America, tribe after tribe gave witness to the fact that they thoroughly believed in their life-styles.

There seems to be no record of subversives, spies or traitors. There were, however, leaders of factions. For example, so determined was a group within the Hidatsa that they split away in anger over an argument and became the Crow of the Plains. But this was not the action of turncoats. With the advent of the white man, one tribe after another went down fighting. The individual members so believed in the values of their

**Right** This Kwakiutl chief holds a broken copper, symbol of the destruction of wealth
**Below** A Northwest Coast fishing camp

**Bottom** A Chilkat blanket. These blankets were woven with mountain goat and puppy dog's hair

**Below** A wolf mask which was carved by a Nootka craftsman sometime in the eighteenth century

**Left** Chief Shake's houseboards. These totemic boards served as a partition to his quarters

**Left** Tlingits arrayed for a
Potlach at Sitka, Alaska
**Below** As the dancers
pulled on concealed strings
the great beaks opened
and slammed shut
**Right** This Kwakiutl chief
holds a "Speakers Staff"
and carved rattle. The
buttons on his blanket
symbolize the coppers to
which he is entitled
**Below right** A Northwest
Coast matriarch. Head
deformation was
considered a mark of
beauty

cultures that they quite often died for them. It is this kind of loyalty that has baffled the one-way minds of missionaries, government planners and social workers for generations.

For all their wealth and their interest in it, with the advent of the white man, Russians first and Americans later, the Northwest Coast Indians faced bankruptcy. Among other things, the United States' authorities had the presumptuousness to ban the Potlatch. Self-appointed social planners saw the custom as insidiously dangerous to the Indians' cultural and economic well-being. And with this directive, typical of the white man's meddling insistence that he always knows what is best for others, the Americans effectively killed the very spirit of the Northwest Coast Indians. This was not only sad, but stupid. The Indians had been making out extremely well for several hundred years on their own. In the event, their culture rotted away like their totem poles in the rain-soaked beaches of the Pacific coast.

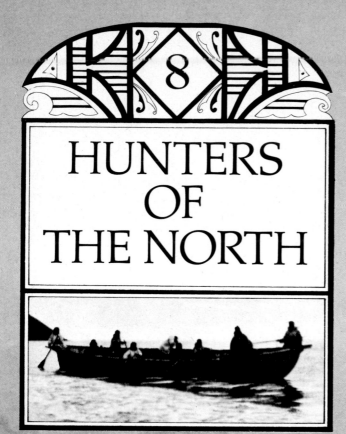

# HUNTERS OF THE NORTH

**8**

The northlands of Canada and Alaska vary not only in terrain, but in flora and fauna. Yet with this variation there is one thing in common—long and frigid winters. This makes for a most harsh and stark environment for all who live there. From the banks of Labrador to the Bering Sea, it was the country of moose and caribou, musk ox and polar bear, walrus and whale. Dense forests in the east stretched west to the barren tundra wastelands of Alaska. This was the land of rugged Indians. And to the far north was the most harsh of all environments, the frozen Arctic, the habitat of the Eskimo.

Algonquian-speaking tribes like the Montagnais and Naskapi occupied territory east of Hudson Bay, while to the west were the Algonquians, the Cree and Saulteaux. The Dog Ribs, Yellowknives, and Hares, the Taltans and Tanaina, Athabascan speakers, lived in the far northwestern parts of Canada and central Alaska.

Among the Algonquians, men were assigned hunting territories to which certain hunters held exclusive use. All manner of devices were employed, bows and arrows, traps, snares and deadfalls. Unlike the communal buffalo hunting of the Plains, most of the hunting was done individually. It was arduous work that required as much patience as it did skill. In winter men hunted on snowshoes. With them they could track a wounded moose for miles and drag home its carcass on a birchbark toboggan.

This north country was the land of the birch tree and from its paperlike bark these people fashioned their graceful canoes, box containers, even conical horns for calling moose. Instead of using hides, they covered their tepees in great sheets of birchbark.

Small boxes designed to hold valuables were often decorated by scraping away the surface of the bark to reveal a darker layer. In this manner the artist produced silhouettelike animal forms. Utilitarian containers were cut in large patterns from pieces of bark, stitched with roots and, as with the canoes, the seams were covered with pitch. Some were used as cooking vessels. When filled with water, heated stones were dropped in to make the water boil. Boiled meat and broth were favorites among all the North American tribes. Stone boiling was commonly utilized by those who made clay cooking pots as well as those who fashioned watertight baskets. The Plains Indians with neither wooden containers, clay pots nor baskets, used

the paunch of a buffalo, supported on stakes, as a receptacle for boiling.

Stone boiling had one minor disadvantage. When the hot stones struck the cold water, a certain amount of flaking occurred which left tiny sandy particles in the water and in turn the broth. And this grit was especially hard on the teeth, wearing them down prematurely.

The birchbark tepee, like its skin counterpart of the Plains, was an amazingly efficient structure. With a smoke hole at the top and the fire pit placed directly below, the conical-shaped dwelling was uniquely functional. In the coldest of weather, the decreased volume of air at the top reduced the amount of heat required to warm the lower living space. The result was that the tepee was entirely comfortable. In a sense, the tepee-dwellers lived warm and snug in their chimneys. Interestingly, the sides of the Plains' hide tepees could be rolled up around the base in summertime, making a veritable parasol of the lodge. The tepee in no matter what region was most ingeniously designed.

Far to the northwest of the Algonquians lived the Athabascan hunters. Their fare was the moose, caribou, musk ox and hare. One tribe, the Hare, depended so heavily on the big rabbit that they were given its name. Owing to the fact that a seven-year epidemic nearly killed out the hares, the designation was hardly a lucky one for the Indians. With the scarcity of game, the people starved.

The Athabascan tribes were loosely divided into hunting bands, each with a prescribed territory. There

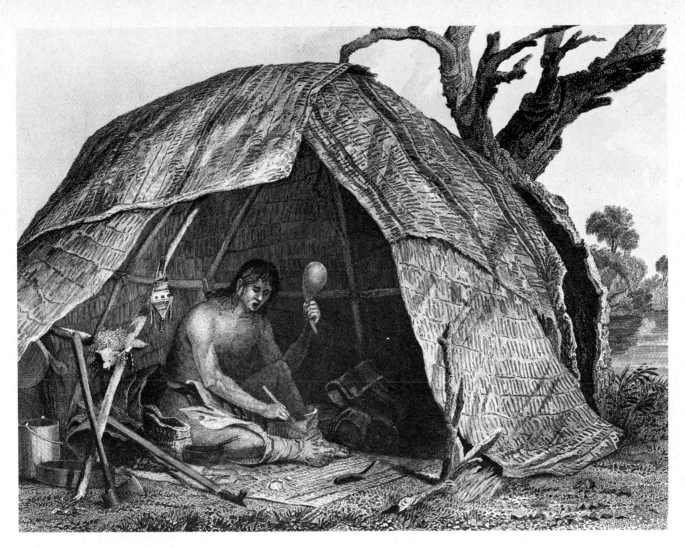

Pages 118-19 Charles Verner's painting of
Woodland Indians in camp **Inset** Eskimo
hunters in a Umiak covered with walrus skin
**Above left** Kutchin men sketched by
Alexander Murray c 1846. These were
Athabascan hunters of the far north
**Left** A painting by T. Davies of an Algonquian
village on the St. Lawrence River **Above** A
shaman making medicine. Sacred songs
accompanied by rattles ensured the efficacy of
the concoction **Below** Interior of a Nova
Scotia wigwam

were no headmen, but during times of conflict a war
chief was appointed. About the only governmental
controls that existed were the decisions rendered by
the elders in settling quarrels in the event recompense
had not been made.

As was the custom with many Indians, women were
confined to a separate hut during the menstrual period
as well as when giving birth. The power of women was
much feared. Among the Plains tribes, for example,
women might not touch a man's weapons, neither his
shield nor his war bonnet lest they become con-
taminated and in turn ineffectual.

Polygamy was commonly practiced by these northern
tribes. Several groups observed a unique method of
settling disputes arising when one man coveted
another man's wife. Very simply, a wrestling match was
organized. The winner won the woman.

Among the world's more ingenious people, the
Eskimo rank high. No man without exceeding wit and
unmatchable courage could hope to survive the deep
and penetrating cold, the endless winter nights of the
inhospitable Arctic. Unbelievably, the Eskimo did it,
and did it very happily.

The Eskimo were as clever as they were cheerful.
Among their inventions were the harpoon and *kayak*,
snow goggles, the dog sled, a stone oil lamp and the

**Above** A painting by Paul Kane shows a Cree
chief displaying his calumet or pipe stem
**Above right** An Eskimo with hunting weapons
and kayak: a painting by John Halkett **Right** A
Cree birch-bark box showing caribou and bear
**Far right** An eskimo mask

**TATTANNÆUK.** *Esquimaux Interpreter, — named by the English in Hudson's Bay* **AUGUSTUS**, *the faithful follower of Captains S.ʳ John Franklin, & S.ʳ Geo. Back, & D.ʳ Richardson, in their Arctic land Expeditions in N. America.*

J. Halkett

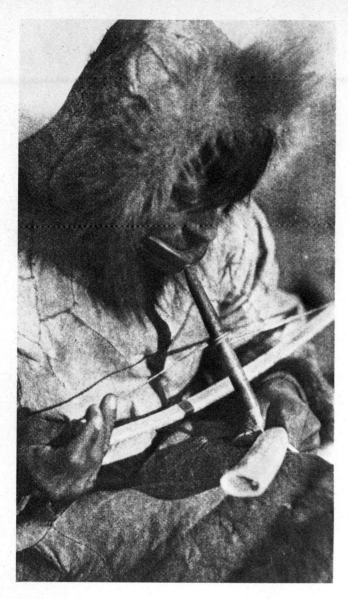

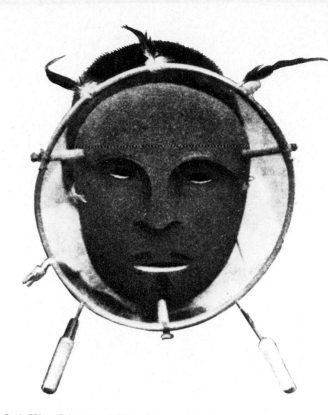

**Left** A King Islander drilling ivory with a bow drill **Above** An Eskimo masked dancer
**Right** An Eskimo woman bejewelled with nose ring and lip beads **Far right** An Eskimo singer from Coronation Gulf, north of Hudson Bay. An ingenious people, the Eskimo have learnt to live with their harsh environment

dome-shaped snowhouse called an *igloo*. The kayak, a skin-covered canoe, was completely decked, which permitted the paddler to roll over and upright himself without fear of either sinking or of even getting wet.

As hunters, the Eskimos' daring and patience were unbeaten. In great skin-covered open boats called *umiaks*, men would go to sea in search of whales and walrus. Harpooning demanded an extremely close approach to these dangerous animals. Hurling the harpoon, a spear with a detachable point, deep into the flesh required accuracy and skill. When struck, whales dived at tremendous speed. To prevent their loss, a long rawhide rope, attached to the point, was equipped with inflated bladders. These little buoys enabled the hunters to keep track of their quarry.

Seals were caught in a similar manner, harpooned by a single hunter in his kayak. Sometimes seals could be surprised sunning themselves on an ice floe, which gave the hunter an advantage in the time it took them to dive into the water.

Hunting through the ice was another method. Seals have several breathing holes hidden from view by the snow. The hunters often depended on their dogs to scent out the location, yet men themselves were often just as capable of discovering the holes by the same technique. Hours, indeed often several days of patient waiting were required before a seal might frequent a hole. When by chance it appeared, the hunter was ready to plunge his harpoon into his prey.

One of the more innovative hunting techniques was especially useful in downing a polar bear or wolf. Here the hunter rolled a strip of baleen or whalebone into a tight coil, the ends of which had been sharpened to a point. This was inserted into a chunk of frozen blubber. The innocent-looking bait was then placed at a spot known to be the haunt of an animal. A wolf, later devouring the morsel, would soon fall prey to the Eskimo's deviousness. The blubber, after a short time in the animal's stomach, would melt, releasing the baleen spring. The sharp ends would puncture the animal's insides and internal bleeding would result. Now the wary hunter had nothing more to do than to follow a trail of blood to his victim.

The Eskimo villages were little more than bands of

hunters. There were no headmen, there was no government. People lived simply by rules of behavior established for generations, rules that demanded the utmost in cooperation and sharing. While a man might hunt alone, he carefully shared his kill with everyone. Someday he might not be so fortunate and would welcome the generosity of a neighbor.

The Eskimos shared everything—tools, clothing, food, dog teams, even their wives. It was expected that a host would offer a visiting guest his woman for the night. It honored not only the woman, but demonstrated the man's generosity. It is true, both he and his wife expected something in return.

Wife sharing, however, in no way implied a looseness in the moral code. Faithfulness in marriage was expected of both sexes. On the other hand, a man enamored of another's wife might plan a tryst. More commonly, however, rather than trying to carry on an affair, he would plot the husband's murder. At the opportune moment, he would stab his victim in the back with his snow knife; Eskimos never fought face to face. Then the lover would abscond with his new

woman to the safety of another village. Relatives of the murdered husband frequently planned revenge, with the result that Eskimo communities were sporadically torn by bloody feuds.

Eskimo religious beliefs were, to say the most, unstructured. They consisted essentially of a horde of busy, morbid and dangerous spirits which were to be avoided at all costs. They brought nothing but trouble, misfortune, sickness and death. Shamans, capable of such marvelous accomplishments as seeing events far away, could also diagnose sickness. Curing a patient meant removing the cause of illness. This the shaman did by ridding the body of splinters of bone or wood previously implanted either by a sorcerer or by the evil spirits themselves.

The Eskimo are an enigmatic people. Surviving most efficiently in the earth's harshest environment, comforted by the world's gloomiest religion, these northern hunters are recognized as among the happiest, most cheerful people of all mankind. Here were the practitioners par excellence of the philosophy "eat, drink and be merry for tomorrow we must die."

125

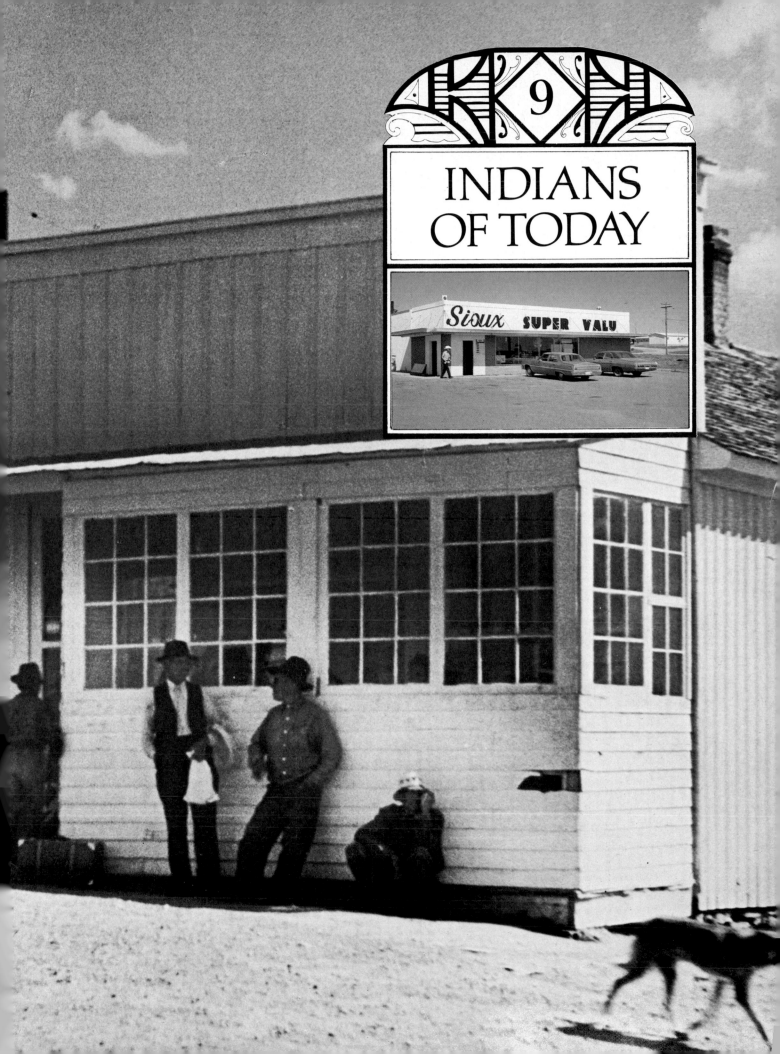

When the last of the frozen bodies were dumped into the mass grave at Wounded Knee, South Dakota, on that chill December day in 1890, an era ended for the American Indian. It was a bloody period marked by skirmishes and battles and wars. For the Indian, it was a time of destruction, death and dishonor.

From Cortez's arrival in 1520 until the massacre at Wounded Knee, the Indians had fought to defend themselves against white encroachment. Some, like the Calusa and the Natchez, Wampanoag and the Massachusetts, were literally annihilated. Others, the Creek and Choctaws, the Shawnee and the Sauk and Fox and many more, were driven from their homelands. Some were grudgingly permitted to remain, tiny islands here and there engulfed by a sea of white men. Such were the Penobscot, the Iroquois and the Powhatans, the Cherokee and the Seminoles.

With the foregoing exceptions, the government's policy was one of complete removal. Andrew Jackson's determination to rid the East of all the Indians was, in fact, a chief executive's response to the nation's temper as a whole. In the 1830s the easy solution to the Indian problem was merely to push the tribes out of sight. The land was now needed not only for white settlement, but it would be put to a much better use.

Far to the west of the Mississippi River, the government carved out a vast piece of land, called it "Indian Territory," and assigned blocks of countryside on which Indians might live. Little or no consideration was given to the Indians whose homelands these new settlers displaced. In the southwestern part of the "Territory" the Five Civilized Tribes were situated.

It was the Cherokee, Creeks, Choctaw, Chicasaw and Seminoles who were called "civilized," and this was chiefly because the Cherokees had an alphabet. Developed by a scholar named Sequoya, presumably the people could read and write their own language.

By the close of the Civil War in the 1860s, other eastern tribes had been removed to Indian Territory. Squeezed into lands reserved for the Five Tribes, Shawnees and Delawares, Sauk and Fox and Senecas, Potawatomis and Osage were granted space. And as the West burgeoned with more and more white settlers clamoring for land, the western states and territories were also anxious to rid themselves of Indians. Midwestern tribes, the Oto and Missouri, the Poncas and Pawnee were "given" land in Indian Territory. So, too, were some of the Plains tribes. The Kiowa and Comanche, the Cheyenne, Arapaho and Wichita were settled on reservations in what is now Oklahoma.

Considerable rhetoric rang through the halls of the United States Congress in the 1870s concerning the "Indian Problem" and the subject of removal. By now the Indians had their champions. Many were sincere do-gooders from Philadelphia and Boston, men and women whose forefathers had successfully wiped out the Indian long, long before. Now, with heart on sleeves, they came to the defense of the noble savage.

But their voices were weak and to little avail. The policy of isolation on reservations prevailed.

Nor is it surprising to observe that in all this shifting of people to satisfy the white man's lust for land, his conviction of a manifest destiny, the Indians were never consulted as to what their own preferences might be.

The Pueblo tribes of the Southwest, and to a degree the Navaho, were the least disturbed of any Indians in the United States. After the revolt in 1680, which among other things taught the Franciscan fathers the advantage of allowing the Indians to retain their religion, the Pueblos were more or less unmolested. Nobody really wanted their desert lands. They carried on much as they had for generations and they still do. Here the men still farm, the women fashion pottery. The Navaho men have become master silversmiths, their women weave striking rugs. Today these are the colorful Indians of the "Land of Enchantment" whose dances tourists crowd to see. But most significant is the fact that these people have retained, and have been permitted to retain, much of their heritage. As such, they are a tribute to Indian determination and the will to survive.

It is interesting to note that of the 370 treaties which the United States Senate ratified with Indian tribes, each one was made to the distinct advantage of the white man. The Sauk and Fox, for instance, got the generous sum of three cents an acre for their territory. Nearly every treaty was broken, but, incredibly, there is no record of the Indians having ever breached a single one of them.

Life on the reservations during the last half of the nineteenth century was grim. Unable any longer to feed themselves, the Indians were given rations. Beef cattle were supplied, which when released from corrals were shot and butchered by the Indians—the whole affair having the semblance of a rodeo buffalo hunt. Rations were, however, often short; short because of the graft of Bureau of Indian Affairs agents and dishonest suppliers. But there were more fundamental problems than the mere sticky fingers of Indian Affairs agents and crooked traders. The philosophy on Indian affairs was based on the simplistic and determined assumption that by remaking of Indians in the image of white men, the Indian problem could be successfully solved. It was a policy formulated by well-meaning church groups, organizations devoted exclusively to the best interests of Indians, working with government policy makers. It contained all the basic elements of the Puritan ethic of the 1870s. It was essentially the American philosophy for success. Industriousness and frugality, thought to be easily achievable for the Indian through farming, made for self-sufficiency and prosperity. Fear of God through

**Preceding pages** Life for the modern Indian: a trading post on the Sioux Reservation and (**inset**) a tribally operated supermarket
**Right** A Navaho woman carries home a sheep

staunch adherence to Christian principles produced men of upright morality and unimpeachable integrity. It was an approach to life that was clear-cut and forthright. And today, from the Indian's point of view, hindsight indicates it was disastrously wrong.

Even with a policy designed by the best-intentioned people, forcing benighted savages into the alien culture of an enlightened and dominant society was about as logical as trying to transform a hawk into a dove.

From the white man's viewpoint, the Indians were savages. They scalped one another and white men too. They killed women and children. They practiced polygamy. The men did not work, rather had fun hunting or sat around the council lodge smoking the evil weed tobacco while their women carried the

burdens, even did the back-breaking work of tilling the fields. Rather than accumulating wealth for a rainy day, they splurged it on feasting, squandered it in gambling or just gave it away. And as if to confirm their savagery, not only did witch doctors and medicine men perform wild ceremonies with rattles and drums to cure the sick, but some men underwent cruel and inhumane self-torture in the Sun Dance, worshipping pagan gods, especially the Sun.

The white man conveniently overlooked the entire gestalt of Indian culture in their blind and determined self-righteousness. They also easily forgot that the English and the French had paid bounties for scalps and that the frontiersmen boasted of the "hair" they had taken. The Yankees were quick to condone the

**Left** Bessie Solomon, a Mississippi Choctaw,
fashions a basket as did her ancestors years ago
**Above** A Comanche beadworker

destruction of the Iroquois villages by General
Sullivan's armies in the eighteenth century, were loud
in their cheers at General Custer's killing of women
and children at the surprise attack on the Cheyennes
at the battle of the Washita a hundred years later. This,
of course, was all done in the name of civilization and
manifest destiny.

For the Puritanical Americans, polygamy was a
frightening and evil thing. Not only was it immoral,
it was unclean. Quite naturally, the Indians must be
perverted. Some not only had two wives, but a good

provider might well maintain six women. Yet the
white man winked at men who supported a mistress,
and surreptitiously upheld the institution of prosti-
tution. And today, to frown on the Indians' practice
of polygamy is even more preposterous. With easy
divorce and quick remarriage, the Americans practice
a form of both serial polygamy and polyandry, not in
having two spouses at a time, but enjoying one after
another. The consequences for the children of a
broken home are devastating, which was not the case
when divorce occurred in the Indian's consanguine
family.

The whole idea that Indian men did not work was
ridiculous. Hunting to insure enough food for the
year-round supply was hard work, a task that required

skill and patience, endurance and courage. It was not a sport as viewed by the white man, but difficult, arduous work. War, too, was a profession for which men trained diligently to become proficient both in the use of weapons and in stratagem. To the white man, however, laboring long hours behind a plow, whose days were often spent in drudgery, an Indian's life appeared idyllic. The white man was jealous.

With the exception of the nomadic buffalo-hunting tribes of the Great Plains, the Indians living east of the Rocky Mountains were all farmers. And the women did the farming. They also carried the firewood, toted the water, shouldered the burdens. Theirs, too, was the strenuous work of tanning hides and the tedious job of making the clothing. When traveling or moving camp, the men led the procession empty-handed, save for their weapons, while the women trailed dutifully behind bearing the provisions. There was good reason for the men to take the lead unencumbered. They must be the scout, the armed protector of their family in the event of a surprise attack. They must be vigilant. In the eyes of the white man, however, the Indian women were relegated to the status of beasts of burden by men too lazy and arrogant to work.

The ceremonies of the Indians, including those involved with curing, were considered as pagan rites conceived by a savage mind. The shaman's antics, his rattling rattles, his singing, his trance appeared demented, childish and ineffective—this, despite the fact that they very often worked. The Sun Dance with its grueling self-torture epitomized the barbarity of Indian mentality. To worship the Sun and other deities was not only polytheism but antichristian, both of which were anathema to the Victorian consciousness. Yet strangely these very white men revered a Saviour who himself endured the torture of crucifixion for their sakes. The Indians were far more direct. They themselves forthrightly suffered to gain power for the benefit of others. Interestingly too, the missionaries who ridiculed the polytheistic beliefs held by the Indians, themselves acknowledged a Holy Trinity and in some instances a Virgin Mother.

The Indians' concepts of property and wealth were diametrically opposed to that of the white men's. For the majority of the tribes, tangible items were accumulated only to be given away. In the Plains, the horse became a standard medium of exchange and a man with a large herd was considered rich. But to obtain respect and status, he had to give his horses away. Generosity was the sure path to social success. It seems that only in California was money, in the form of shells, accumulated for money's sake.

For the Indian, the route to prestige lay in one's ability to acquire property and then share it with others. The epitome of this concept was the Potlatch as

A feast takes place at the Flathead Reservation in Montana. Many of the old customs and traditions survive

practiced in the Northwest. Here the give-away reached the proportions of mayhem. But the point to be understood is that for Indians, property for property's sake, wealth for wealth's sake, had in itself no meaning. On the other hand, property and wealth, when shared, when given away, were vital to the individual's chance for gaining the respect of his fellow men, of achieving for himself status and prestige. The white man's approach to property and money was quite different. Earning money not only brought the comforts of life, but large amounts could bring especially desirable rewards. Wealthy men could afford mansions and servants, join exclusive clubs, bedeck their wives in emeralds. If they were to receive the accolade of public recognition, they had best contribute to the building funds for the new library or give heavily to the church. Yet the wealthy man's real status, the awe of the public's acclaim in the nineteenth

century was and still is based upon the very aura of his being rich. His money brought him all the good things of life, he was envied, he was held in high regard. The rich man was reverently respected yet somewhat resented for the mere size of his bank account. In the nineteenth century, money was god. The Americans did not then, nor have not now, equated success with much else than the dollar sign.

Because of the white man's ignorance, misunderstanding, inconsistent thinking and blatant prejudice, national policy in the 1870s demanded that Indian culture be changed to conform with Christian standards of values, with the "white" methods of doing things. The Indians had been defeated militarily, now they were to be destroyed culturally.

Indian children were sent to boarding schools, often far from their homes. Here they were dressed in uniforms. The boys' hair was cut short. They were taught the conventional reading, writing and arithmetic. If they were caught speaking their native tongue, they were physically punished, best accomplished by a strapping with a leather belt on a naked back.

On the reservation, land was parceled out to each family head in 160-acre tracts. What reservation land was not allotted was either retained in tribal ownership or sold to white settlers. Indian men were given plows and horses and told to farm their allotments. In spite of instructors provided by the government to teach the Indians the techniques of agriculture, the plan never really worked. Crops failed and the men's interest waned. This was only natural. Farming was a woman's work.

Missionaries early came to the reservations vying with one another to save souls. Church groups saw to it that the Sun Dance was banned and polygamy

abolished. Shamans went into hiding. With these disruptions, Indian culture was all but killed.

Beginning in the latter part of the nineteenth century, governmental policy was administered by a specially created office, the Bureau of Indian Affairs. Charged with the responsibility of transforming the Indian into a replica of the white man thereby helping him to become a productive and adjusted member of the wider society, the Bureau operated schools, hospitals, and provided a series of social services.

One branch of the Bureau concerned itself with the Indian's property—land. Reservations were not concentration camps as is often mistakenly believed, but rather land reserved for the Indians as part of the treaty agreements. Early policy makers, aware that the Indians would be fleeced of their holdings by greedy white settlers, decreed that the land should be held in trust. Thus, the Indians might not sell their land without permission of the guardian. Even the leasing of land was supervised by the Bureau. As the years went by, pressure from both Indians and whites caused the Bureau to sell both tribally and individually owned portions. Today only some 55 million acres remain in trust.

Though often maligned, in general the Bureau has been staffed by dedicated men and women who sincerely devote themselves to the welfare of their wards. Criticism is unfairly directed at the Bureau because of its obvious failure to bring the Indian people to a sound economic and viable social level. And it can be said with little fear of contradiction that the Indians have the highest death rate, the highest infant mortality, the highest rate of alcoholism, the most suicides and the lowest incomes of any group of Americans. To the civil service employees of the Bureau—middle-class teachers and doctors, social workers and farm agents, all with good middle-class aspirations—it is disappointing and frustrating.

In 1924, Congress granted Indians citizenship, a presumptuous gratuity indeed from a nation to the very people whose homeland it really is. Again, in 1935, Congress passed the Indian Reorganization Act, a magnanimous bill which recognized that the Indian

tribes, as soveriegn nations within the nation, were entitled to the right of self-government. This, too, was an overdue apology from an overbearing conqueror. In principle, the tribes were now allowed to rule themselves, draw up constitutions, elect tribal councilmen, appoint judges and tribal police. There was only one flaw. The constitutions were prepared in Washington by well-meaning bureaucrats versed in the laws of the white man. No one thought of consulting the Indians. The result was that it required considerable propaganda to convince many of the tribes to adopt the provisions in referendums. But the over-all idea was thought to be a sound one—it was going to do good for Indians whether they understood it or not.

Reservations were either situated on lands originally occupied by Indians or lands they received in exchange for that which they had ceded. Treaty provisions specified that Indians would pay no taxes on their lands. Indians may, of course, impose taxes on land or for other purposes if they so desire. None have done so to this day. Indians are subject to all applicable state and federal taxes, including income tax, and are eligible for all social services available to non-Indians, including aid to dependent children and unemployment insurance.

In an endeavor to rectify the unconscionably low prices paid to Indians for their lands, the government instituted an Indian Claims Commission. Here tribes could bring their cases for hearing and many were idemnified with millions of dollars. After a century of dishonor, the Americans were making restitutions.

Beginning in the mid-1930s and continuing to this date, studies and surveys were conducted in the field by teams of anthropologists, educators, psychologists all to the end of understanding the Indian problem, all in the hope of determining what might be done to improve his lot. Books and reports were written by the ream, glowing programs of self-help were planned in Washington. But again, an important factor was overlooked. Seldom were the Indians consulted. Most Indians did not understand all the complexities of the imposed programs and consequently failures outnumbered successes.

One such plan called for the urbanization of Indians. Since opportunities for employment on or near the reservations were all but nonexistent, it was believed that a program of relocation would enhance the Indian's chance of gaining a cash income through work in metropolitan centers. Indians were reimbursed to make the move and employment for them was arranged. Many remained in the cities, yet many more, ill-prepared emotionally for city life or poorly qualified for the jobs to which they were assigned, returned discouraged to their reservations.

The idea of bringing industry to the reservations was tried. This would enable Indians to find employment at home. In some instances the idea proved successful. For example, Congress established the Indian Arts and Crafts Board for the purpose of reviving fading Indian arts to the economic and cultural benefit of the Indians. The crafts that exist today are in large measure thanks to the efforts both of that board and the Indians, who themselves wished to preserve something of their heritage. Other attempts at local industry were less successful. The monotonous regimen required of belt-line mass production was sometimes more than Indians were able to stand. And unfortunately, the rate of Indian unemployment is still the highest in the nation.

It almost seemed that in spite of the government's help, the services, the protections, the plans and programs, the Indians, in defiance, neither sank nor swam—they just floated. And neither the bureaucrats nor the social scientists, with all their resources and knowledge, could fathom the mystery. That was simply because they had overlooked the key.

The Indians, militarily defeated, their culture destroyed, were a people without a spirit, without a will. They could easily see that their way of life was no match for the militarily superior, industrially powerful nation of white men. Even their religion had failed them. Its "power" was weak as evidenced by their defeat. They were a people embarrassed and ashamed. Pride in their heritage completely vanished. By the 1930s, what knowledge of the past that did exist was fading with the passing of the older generation, a generation for which the younger Indians had little respect. By now the plight of the Indians was a national tragedy and disgrace, a direct consequence of a concerted effort at genocide, both physical and cultural. No amends, however beneficent, no amount of governmental aid, no amount of scientific social planning seemed to be able to heal the wounds.

And then, beginning in the 1960s, something happened. Here and there a handful of educated Indians, often independently, sometimes in concert with students of Indian affairs, began to recognize not only the value of Indian culture, but the desperate need for preserving Indian heritage in order that their people might once again enjoy a sense of self-respect. Only by a feeling of pride in his heritage, only in an attitude of dignity could the Indian hope to raise himself from a state of malaise and apathy to a position of achievement and prosperity. This was the key the bureaucrats had missed, this was the puzzle the social scientists could not put together.

The well-meaning efforts of the Congress and Bureau officials, of organizations like the Indian Rights Association of Philadelphia and the Association of American Indian Affairs of New York City had not gone for naught.

When America was first discovered, it is thought there were approximately one million native Americans. By 1900 their numbers were reduced to an estimated 300,000. Today, however, with improved health conditions over the last half century, the Indian population is again reaching the million mark. Conditions on the reservations are markedly improved since the 1930s. Many of the programs are taking effect, but strangely, it is the Indians themselves who conceived and spearheaded the drive toward renewed Indian self-respect.

D'Arcy McNickle, a Flathead Indian who once won himself a Rhodes scholarship and has written several provocative books on Indian affairs, both fiction and nonfiction, formed an organization called American Indian Development. Its purpose was twofold, each of which was novel. One was to meet with Indian groups, discuss with them what they themselves felt was needed in their communities, not what some social planner in Washington thought was good for them, and proceed to assist them in achieving their goal. While this approach had never been used before, the results were both positively tangible and significantly productive in their potential for building morale. The Navahos at Crown Point, New Mexico, for example, concluded that they needed a community hall combined with a laundromat. The bureaucrats frowned on the idea as an unnecessary luxury. Ten miles of paved road would be more civilized. But the Navahos persevered. With the aid of a small grant from a foundation, they built their community house themselves and bought their washing machines. Now the women could do their laundry while the men counciled. All this may appear a very minor matter, but it was a major step in changing the national concept in dealing with Indians, a very sound step in developing Indian self-determination.

The second purpose of AID was to establish among young Indians a sense of self-respect for their heritage; it is the youth, after all, who hold the future of Indian self-expression in America. While more and more young Indians were attending colleges, the rate of dropouts was dangerously high. To combat this unfortunate situation, summer workshops were developed. Here Indian students were given a crash course in Indian heritage and culture, the object being to give them a solid background of their own so they might face their white competitors on an equal

On an upright loom Bertha Stevens beats the weft in her Navaho rug with a wooden comb

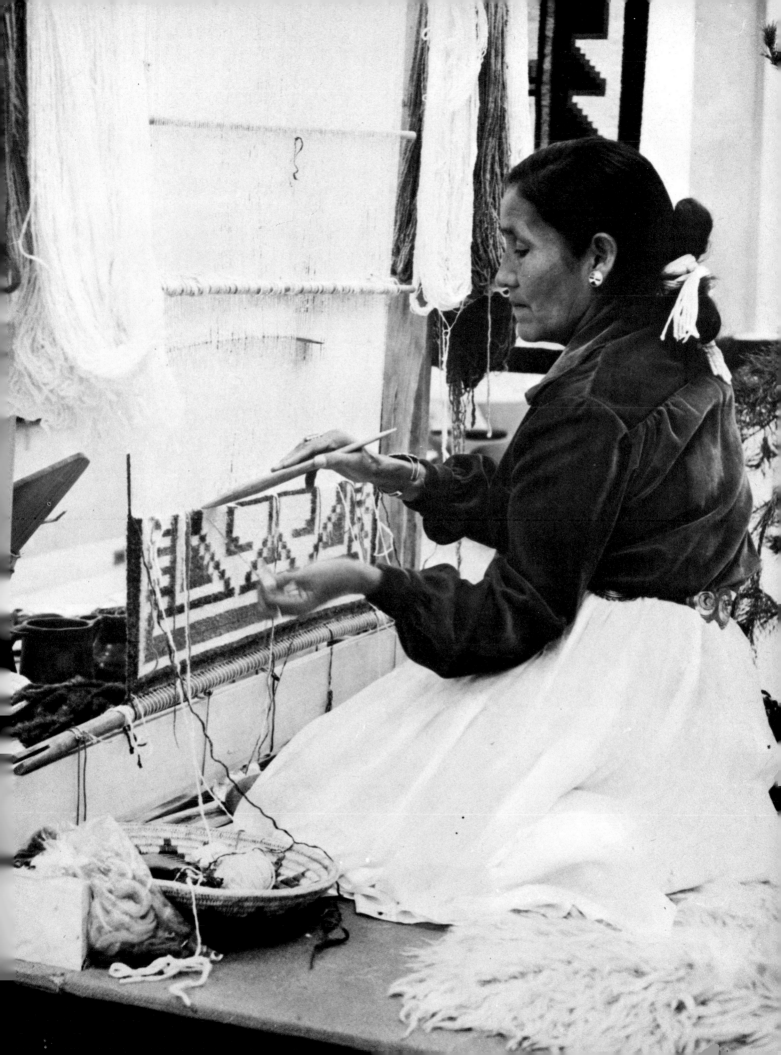

psychological footing. It worked. Dropouts decreased, other workshops were established and today young Indians are attending colleges and universities in relatively large numbers and, moreover, remaining to graduate.

Lloyd New, a Cherokee, whose forefathers had been removed to Indian Territory, had a growing awareness that the only hope for Indians to survive the white man's cultural onslaught lay in their having a proper regard for their own heritage. In accepting a position as director of the Indian School in Santa Fe, New Mexico, in the 1960s, he did it on the condition that its curriculum emphasize American Indian culture in all its ramifications, Indian art in its broadest perspective.

**Left** Drying meat on the Great Plains
**Right** A Fort Hall Shoshoni takes a respite from mowing hay

Now named the Institute of American Indian Art, it offers, in addition to the regularly accepted academic courses, training in Indian painting, sculpture, weaving, music, dance, history, language—the entire gamut of Indian culture. Graduates are proving to be productive, positive, enthusiastic citizens, capable of functioning in two worlds—that of the white man and, with great pride, that of the Indian. Whereas before this nation had been educating young Indians to be at best something less than individuals, now the Institute is offering the young Indian information about his heritage, his people's achievements and contributions.

At the same time, men and women on the reservations began remembering the old traditions, reviving the ancient ceremonies. Among the Sioux, for example, the Sun Dance is again being performed. The Mandans requested and received the return of one or more of their sacred medicine bundles from a prestigious museum in New York. The Sarsi of Alberta are requesting bundles from the Provincial Museum of Alberta so that they may preserve their ceremonial practices for their self-betterment. The Pueblos and Navahos, of course, have been able to retain their ceremonial life almost intact since the time of Spanish contact, but a new and exciting development has recently taken place. Whereas formerly the Navaho medicine man's practices were frowned upon by federal medical authorities as mere primitive mumbo jumbo, now government physicians are working in close harmony with native doctors to effect a cure.

Other actions, of a most constructive nature, have recently occurred. The Zunis have taken over complete control of all their tribal affairs. The Navahos have established a college with Indian administrators, faculty and students. Vine Deloria's book, *Custer Died For Your Sins*, is impressive, significant of the well-written books on Indian affairs being published by responsible Indian authors.

This is good. But only when all Indian children whether in public or federally operated Indian schools are given thorough training in their cultural heritage will Indians be able to achieve a full sense of belonging, an enthusiastic pride in what they can contribute. Public schools have been particularly derelict in their failure to teach anything about minority cultures. Besides the more ambitious curriculum of the Institute of Indian Art, the schools operated by the Bureau of Indian Affairs now offer token courses in Indian heritage and language. It now behooves Congress to acquaint itself with Indian Affairs, to appropriate funds and direct the Bureau to expand the curriculum of the Indian schools and subsidize public schools which Indians attend so that they, too, may give courses in Indian enrichment. Only with a feeling of self-respect, of pride in their heritage and the security of dignity can the Indians, or in reality anyone else, effectively participate in a positive manner within American society.

Despite the recent progress by Indians in self-determination, the advances in educational philosophy, their increasing sense of self-respect, the patience of a small number of youthful Indians would not be contained. Resentful of past wrongs, groups of young people rallied themselves under the banner of Red Power. Other urbanized activists organized themselves formally as the American Indian Movement. They were convinced that the "Uncle Tomahawks" on the reservations were pawns of the Bureau of Indian Affairs and doing nothing for their people's well-being. In the late winter of 1972, the leaders of AIM, in the hope of bringing the Indians' grievances against the Bureau before the American public, took it upon themselves to capture the little town of Wounded Knee. Choosing the site of the massacre of Sioux ghost dancers in 1890 was astute. Wounded Knee is the symbol of the white man's former cruelty toward Indians, his past disregard for their way of life.

The directors of AIM, in taking over at Wounded Knee, made several demands including the removal of the duly elected Sioux tribal chairman and the return to the Sioux of all tribal lands as of the Treaty of 1868. This encompassed all the land of North and South Dakota east of the Missouri River, as well as parts of Wyoming and Nebraska.

AIM received amazing television, newspaper and magazine publicity for its capture of the little hamlet. Wounded Knee became an armed camp. Most of its residents, Indians and whites, were overnight evacuated or fled, to be replaced by young armed Indians. The directors of AIM, self-appointed spokesmen for the Sioux, and indeed for all Indians, continued their demands. Negotiations with federal authorities faltered, the government officials refusing to confer at gunpoint. Blockades were constructed, army tanks were brought in, and the AIM people were themselves besieged. As the days turned into weeks, two federal agents were shot, one permanently paralyzed, and two Indians were killed. The defenders, some wearing feathers as a sign of something from the past about which they knew little and were entitled to even less, took it upon themselves to pillage and burn the trading post, loot the small museum containing many valuable Sioux historical objects and, worse still, loot the homes of the Sioux residents of Wounded Knee.

The tragedy of the 1972-73 episode at Wounded Knee was that even after the 70 days of confrontation, little, if anything, was resolved.

For the Indian, the road to so-called civilization, with its mixed and very questionable blessings, has not been easy. The facts of life are that the Indian has no choice but to exist within the world of the white man. That the mood of the nation has at long last recognized the value of its Indian heritage, has finally assumed a compassionate approach to the affairs of Indians and has belatedly acknowledged the importance of a plurality of life-styles in America, is encouraging. More important, the fact that once again Indians are standing up for their rights betokens nothing but mutual good.

A White River Apache passes the time of day

# SUGGESTED READING

*The Book of the Eskimos* by Peter Freuchen. Crest. Fawcett World.

*The Blackfeet: Raiders on the Northwestern Plains* by John Ewers. Univ. of Oklahoma Press, 1958.

*Bury My Heart at Wounded Knee* by Dee Brown. Holt, Rinehart & Winston, 1971.

*The Cheyenne Indians; their History & Ways of Life* by George Bird Grinnell. Cooper Square, 1923.

*The Comanches, Lords of the South Plains* by Ernest Wallace & E. Adamson Hoeble. Univ. of Oklahoma Press, 1952.

*Creek Indians of Taskigi Town* by Frank G. Speck. Kraus Reprint Organisation, 1908.

*The Crow Indians* by Robert Lowie. Holt, Rinehart & Winston.

*Custer Died for Your Sins* by Vine Deloria. Macmillan, 1970.

*The Hopi Way* by L. Thompson & A. Joseph. Russell & Russell, 1944.

*Indians of the U.S.* by Clark Wissler. Natural History Press.

*Indians of the U.S. Four Centuries of their History & Culture* by Clark Wissler. Doubleday, 1966.

*The Indians of the Southeastern U.S.* by John Swanton. Greenwood, 1946.

*The Last Trek of the Indians* by Grant Foreman. Russell & Russell 1946.

*Laughing Boy* by Oliver LaFarge. Houghton Mifflin Co., 1963.

*The League of the Iroquois* by L. H. Morgan. Franklin, 1902.

*The Navaho* by D. C. Leighton & C. Kluckhohn. Harvard Univ. Press, 1946.

*Osages; Children of the Middle Waters* by John J. Mathews. Univ. of Oklahoma Press, 1961.

*The Sioux: Life & Customs of a Warrior Society* by Royal B. Hassrick. Univ. of Oklahoma Press, 1964.

*The Ten Grandmothers* by Alice Marriott. Univ. of Oklahoma Press, 1945.

# INDEX

Acoma 20, 30
Alabama, The 52
Algonquian 35, 37, 38, 40, 55, 118, 120, *120*
Anasazi 11, 20, 21, 30
Apache 11, 22, *23*, *26–27*, 29, 30, 97, *142*
Apalachee 13, 32
Arapaho *66*, 74, 83, 86, 128
Arikara *64*, 70 74, 79
Assiniboin *73*, 74, *75*, 78
Atakapa 52
Athabascan 11, 22, 118, 120–21
Aztec 13

Bannocks 95
Barlow, Arthur Capt. 32
Bartlett, John R. *96*
Basketmakers 20
Biloxi, The 52
Blackfeet 70, 74, *76–77*
Black Hawk 58, *59*, 59
Bodmer, Karl *66*, *68*, *75*, *76–77*
Brant, Joseph 40, *43*

Caddo 13, 29, 52, *52–53*, 62, 70
Calusa 32, 128
Carson, Kit Colonel 30
Catlin, George *46–47*, 47, 49, *64*, *65*
Cayuga 38
Chaco Canyon *12–13*
Cheedobau *55*
Cherokee 13, 38, 40, *44*, 46, 47, 59, 128, 140
Cheyenne 74, 83, 86, 128, 131
Chickasaw 40, 47, 58, 128
Chilkat 107, *110*, *115*
Chiricahua 30
Chitimacha 13, 52
Choctaw 40, *46–47*, 47, 58, 128, *130*
Cliff Dwellers 20
Cochise 9, 18, 30
Coeur d' Alene 95
Comanche 53, 74, 82, 97, 128, *131*
Coronado, Francisco de Vasques 29
Crazy Horse 83, 86, 87
Cree, The 74, 118, *122*, *123*
Creeks 13, 32, 40, 43, 46, 47, 58, 59, 128
Crow 70, *71*, 74, *78*, 79, 113
Cune Shote *44*, 47
Custer, George A. General 83, 86, 87, 131

Delaware, The 35, 37, 38, 40, 128

de Leon, Ponce 32
Deloria, Vine 140
Denton, William 83, *84–85*
de Oñate, Juan 29, 30
Dog Ribs 118
Ducks *64*

Erie 38
Eskimo 118, *118*, 121, *123*, 124–25, *124*, *125*
Etowa *1*, 5

Flatheads 95, *97*, *101*, *132–33*, 138
Fox *49*, 55, *54–55*, 58, 128

Geronimo 30, *31*

Haida 105, *105*
Hares 118, 120
Hastobiga 28
Havasupai *94–95*, 95
Hiawatha 38
Hidatsa *68*, 70, 74, 113
Hohokam *10*, 11, 12, 18
Hopi 20, 21, *22*
Hurons 40

Illinois, The 38, 55, 58
Iowa, The *54–55*
Iroquois 38, 40, *41*, *42*, 45, 128, 131

Jarvis, John *59*
Jackson, Andrew General 46, 47, 128

Kachina 18, *19*
Kane, Paul 70, *71*, *78*, *101*, *110*, *111*, *122*
Kansa 53
Key Marco, Florida *8*, 9
Kichai 62
Kickapoo 55
Kiowa 74, 82, 128
Kwakiutl *108–9*, *111*, *113*, *117*

Le Moyne, Jacques *34–35*
Leni Lenapi 35

McNickle, D'Arcy 138
Malaspino, Alexander *104*
Mandan *65*, *66*, *68*, 70–74, 82, 140
Manhatts 37
Maricopa *98*

Massachusetts, The 128
Mayan 13
Menomini 55
Mesa Verde National Park *6–7*
Metacom (King Philip) 38
Miami, The 38, 55
Miles, Nelson General 30, 98
Mimbres 9, 12
Missouri, The 53, 128
Mogollan 11, 12, 18
Mohave *99*
Mohawks 37, 38, 43
Mohegans 38
Molehausen, H.B. *24–25*
Montagnais 118

Nahl, C.C. 90, *92–93*
Naite (Chief of San Carlos Apaches) 20, *21*
Naragansets 38
Naskapi 118
Natchez, The 13, 49–50, *50*, *51*, 52, 58, 128
Navaho 11, *14*, *15*, 20, 22–28, *28*, *29*, 30, 128, *129*, *134*, 138, *139*, 140
New, Lloyd 140
Nez Perce 95, 98, *101*
Nootka 105, 106, *110–11*, *115*

Oglethorpe, James 46
Ojibwa 55
Omaha, The 53, 63
Oneida 38, 40
Onondaga 38
Opechancanough 34
Osage *48*, *52–53*, 55, 59, 128
Oto *49*, 53, *55*, 128

Paiute 87, 88, *90*, *91*, 95, 97
Palouse 98
Pamlico 32, *33*, 40
Papago 18, 30, *95*, *97*, *99*
Parsins, F. *44*, 47
Pawnee 53, 62, *62–63*, 66, 70, 74, 128
Pequots 37–38
Penn, William 35
Penobscot 32, 128
Pima 18, 20, 30, *96*, *98*
Pocahontas 34, *39*
Pomeiok 32, *36*
Pomo *96*
Ponca 53, 63, 128
Potawatomis 128
Powhatan 32, 34, 35, 38, 52, 128
Primero, Narbona 20
Pueblo *10*, 11, *11*, 12, *18*, 20, 21–22, 24, 27, 28, 29, 30, 91, 128, 140

Quapaw 53

Red Cloud 79, 83
Remington, Frederic *4*, *5*, *61*, 62, *66* 67, 87
Rolfe, John 34
Russell, Charles *2–3*, 5, *72–73*, *80–81*

Santo Domingo *14*
Sarsi 140
Sauk *49*, 55, *54–55*, 58, 59, 128
Saulteaux 118
Seminole *47*, 47, 128, *134*
Seneca 38, 43, 128
Shalakos 18, *19*
Shawnee 38, 128
Shoshoni 88, *92–93*, 97, 98, 103, *136–37*, *141*
Sioux 52, 53, 55, 59, 63, 72, 74, *74*, *75*, 77, 78, *80*, 82, 83, 86, 87, 102, *126–27*, 140, *141*
Simpson, William *102*, 103
Sitting Bull 83, *83*, 87
Smith, John Capt. 32, 34
Spiro 12, *13*
Sullivan, John 38, 40, 131
Susquahanna 38

Taltans 118
Tanaina 118
Taos Pueblo *16–17*, 18
Tawehash 62
Tawoconi 62
Timuca *34–35*
Tlingit 105, *116*, *135*
Toltec 13
Tsimshian 105
Tunica 32, 52
Tuscarora 38, 40

Umatilla 97
Utes 97, *100*

Vanderlyn, John *32*
Vener, Charles *118–19*, 121

Waco 62
Wampanoag 37, 38, 128
Wappinger 37
Washaki, Chief 98, 103, *103*
Washo 96
Webber, John *110–11*
White, John 32, *33*, *36–37*, 40
Wichita, The 29, 62, *63*, 128
Wimar, Charles 47
Winnebago 55, 59
Wright, Mary Irvin *86–87*

Yellowknives 118
Yuchi 46
Yuma, The *88*

Zuni 14, *15*, 18, *19*, 20, 21, 28, 29, 30, 140

# ACKNOWLEDGEMENTS

This book owes its completion to the help of many people and special thanks are due to each librarian, curator, photographer and secretary who took the trouble to search out illustrative material. Moreover, the author is particularly grateful for the inspiration which many mentors have given and the list is long:

The late Willard Beatty, the late James Blackhorse and his late wife Alice Brings the White Buffalo, Peter Bordeaux, Samuel Broken Leg, Black Medicine or Coffee, Ruth Muskrat Bronson, William Crow, Little Day, Vine Deloria, Bee Garner, A. Irving Hallowell, the late Edward Hayden, Robert Hart, Wade Head, the late Mary Inkanish, the late Chief Iron Shell and his late sister Blue Whirlwind, Charles Kills Enemy, the late Chief Leader Charge, Joseph McCaskill, Sudder McKeel, Robert McKennon, Jane McLaughlin, D'Arcy McNickle, Gordon Macgregor, Dorothy Field Maxwell, Alice Marriott, Nellie Menard, Lloyd New, Helen Peterson, Vincent Price, Rattling Blanket Woman, Irene and Mary Red Shirt, Rose Running Horse, Howard Rock, Richard Tall Bull, Peter Segano, Donald Scott, the late Frank G. Speck, Leslie Speer, Mable Standing Soldier and Clark Wissler.

The author particularly appreciates the help in typing and editing given by Barbara Hassrick.

Each of the foregoing individuals have contributed to this book and any value it may have will be due in large measure to their wisdom. Each is a student of Indian affairs and many are themselves Indians. This book endeavors to encompass something of their comprehension, understanding and good will. This, however, in no way relieves the author of any responsibility for the contents of this work.

The author and publishers are also grateful to the following for the illustration content of this book.
*University of Alaska Museum, Fairbanks:* page 110 (left). *American Museum of Natural History:* pages 1, 9 (bottom), 66 (right), 75, 101 (top), 104–5. *Amon Carter Museum:* pages 2–3, 72–3, 80–1. *Archives of the Legislative Building, Victoria, Canada:* page 108. *Bancroft Library, University of California:* pages 100 (bottom), 116 (top). *British Museum:* pages 33, 36, 37, 40 (top). *John Carter Brown Library, Brown University, Providence, Rhode Island:* page 96 (bottom). *Bureau of Indian Affairs, US Department of the Interior, Washington:* pages 127 (inset), 129, 132–3, 134 (bottom). *National Museum of Canada, Ottawa:* page 125 (right). *William L. Clements Library, University of Michigan:* pages 56–7. *University of Colorado Museum:* page 10 (top right). *Denver Art Museum:* pages 11, 14 (top), 15 (top & bottom), 16–17, 24 (bottom), 38, 40 (bottom), 45 (bottom), 72 (bottom), 80 (bottom), 96 (top left), 111 (bottom), 114, 115 (top & bottom), 123 (bottom left), 134 (top left). *Denver Museum of Natural History:* pages 7 (above), 9 (top), 10 (bottom), 96 (top right). *Denver Public Library:* Jacket, front and back, Front endpapers, back endpapers, 4, 5, 23, 28, 46, 60–1, 64, 65 (top), 66 (left), 67, 68 (top, center, bottom), 70 (top), 71, 74, 76–7, 78 (bottom left & right), 79 (right, top & bottom), 87 (bottom), 88, 89, 94, 97 (right), 98–9, 109 (left & right), 112 (top & bottom), 113 (bottom), 116 (bottom), 117 (top), 118 (inset), 124 (left & right), 125 (left), jacket front and back flap. *The National Gallery of Canada:* pages 43 (left), 120 (bottom). *Thomas Gilcrease Institute of American History and Art:* pages 41, 44, 49 (left), 59, 92–3. *Glenbow Alberta Institute, Calgary:* page 111 (top), 118–19. *William Harmsen Collection, Denver:* page 65 (bottom). *Henry Francis du Pont Winterthur Museum, Wilmington, Delaware:* page 48. *Hudson's Bay Company, Winnipeg:* pages 120 (top), 123 (top). *Indian Arts and Crafts Board, US Department of the Interior:* pages 14 (bottom), 130, 134 (top right), 135, 139. *Library of Congress, Washington:* pages 34, 35 (top & bottom), 42, 43 (right), 45 (top), 49 (right), 121 (top). *Gordon Macgregor, Jekyll Island, Georgia:* pages 126–7, 131, 136–7, 140, 141, 142. *Metropolitan Museum of Art:* pages 68–9. *Museum of the American Indian/Heye Foundation:* pages 10 (top left), 90, 91. *National Gallery of Art, Washington:* page 123 (bottom right). *Peabody Museum, Harvard University:* pages 51, 73 (bottom), 102. *University Museum, University of Pennsylvania:* page 8. *Popperfoto:* page 6 (left). *Royal Ontario Museum, Toronto:* page 70 (bottom), 78 (top), 101 (bottom left & right), 110 (right), 121 (bottom), 122. *St. Louis Art Museum:* page 47 (top). *Smithsonian Institution, National Anthropological Archives, Bureau of American Ethnology Collection:* pages 12–13, 18, 19, 20, 21, 22, 26–7, 29, 31, 39, 47 (bottom), 50 (top & bottom), 52–3, 54, 55, 62–3, 79 (left, top & bottom), 83, 86, 95 (top), 97 (left), 100 (top), 103, 106–7 (top & bottom), 113 (top). *Southwest Museum, Los Angeles:* page 85 (inset). *Stovall Museum of Science and History, University of Oklahoma:* page 13. *Vancouver Public Library:* page 117 (bottom). *Museum für Völkerkunde, Berlin:* pages 24–5. *Wadsworth Atheneum, Hartford:* page 32. *Whitney Gallery of Art, Cody, Wyoming:* pages 84–5. *Yale University Library, New Haven:* page 104.